good dogs
GOOD GOD

Darcey Beale

All scripture quotations, unless otherwise indicated, are taken from The Holy Bible, New International Version® NIV® Copyright © 1973 1978 1984 2011 by Biblica, Inc. ™ Used by permission. All rights reserved worldwide.

Scripture quotations marked (ESV) are from the ESV® Bible (The Holy Bible, English Standard Version®), copyright © 2001 by Crossway, a publishing ministry of Good News Publishers. Used by permission. All rights reserved.

Scripture quotations marked (KJV) are taken from the Authorized (King James) Version. Rights in the Authorized Version in the United Kingdom are vested in the Crown. Reproduced by permission of the Crown's patentee, Cambridge University Press.

Scripture quotations marked (NLT) are taken from the Holy Bible, New Living Translation, copyright ©1996, 2004, 2015 by Tyndale House Foundation. Used by permission of Tyndale House Publishers, a Division of Tyndale House Ministries, Carol Stream, Illinois 60188. All rights reserved.

Scripture quotations marked (CEV) are from the Contemporary English Version Copyright © 1991, 1992, 1995 by American Bible Society, Used by Permission.

Name: Darcey Beale
Title: good dogs: GOOD GOD/ By Darcey Beale
Identifiers: ISBN: 978-1-952369-24-7
Subjects: 1. Body, Mind, Spirit / Inspirational and Personal Growth
2. Biography & Autobiography / Personal Memoirs

Published by EA Books Publishing, a division of
Living Parables of Central Florida, Inc. a 501c3

EABooksPublishing.com

DEDICATION

To my dear Father God,

You walked with me and Ed for years, then brought us Nash to enjoy. You inspired my mind with more doggie-parables, than I could keep up with. I'm overwhelmed by how you comforted me by confirming the message. Without your assistance, I couldn't have finished a thought, much less this book. Thank you for loving me so well. I want to shout it from the rooftops: ***you are real and you are a GOOD GOD!***

CONTENTS

FORWARD i

Comfort Dog...1

No More Death Row 3

Foster Dog 5

Black-Eyed Susans...7

Ed Keeps Watch...9

A Bad Moment...11

Welcome Home, Nash 14

A Bark in the Night...16

Don't Die Before Your Time 18

Blue Water 20

A Dog's Purpose..23

Hungry Dog 25

Goodbye, Sweet Marie...27

Nash Loves What We Hate 29

Forgive Quickly 31

Bad Hair Days..33

Nash Trusts Me...35

Jumping Cat 37

Nash's Stains..39

Don't Take Your Dog for Granted...41

Pet Names and Nicknames..43

Poor Nabi..45

Bellyaches and Heartaches...47

Rescuers Rescue...49

Skunked Again! 51

'Nashing Through the Snow 53

Stinging Flies..55

Nash's Treasure 57

Funniest Thing...59

Stop, Drop and Roll 61

Trees, Marvelous Trees..63

God Interrupts...65

Unreachable Itch 67

Walking Pets...69

Dog Perfume...71

Look at My Dog!..73

Special Chair...75

Who Is Walking Whom?...77

Traded for a Bone 79

Why Worry? 81

Shuffle Your Feet.. 83

Welcome, Stranger... 85

Brain Transplant.. 87

Dogs Face East.. 89

What's Got Into Him?... 91

When Fear Fades.. 93

The Hardest Lap... 95

How to give your life to Jesus Christ 97

If you prayed to receive Christ today: 98

Photos 100

ACKNOWLEDGMENTS... 126

FORWARD

My dogs have taught me so much about the kindness of God. My hope is that these doggie-parables will lead to a better understanding of God, and that someone will move closer to Him through them. My goal with this quirky devotional is to paint an accurate, beautiful picture of God and His good news — although I feel much like a tiny ant attempting to describe a huge skyscraper.

Ironically, I am the last person to ever write a book about dogs or God. Devastated by the death of my beloved dog, Shag, as a little girl, I made a vow not to fall in love with another dog, which I kept long after I was married with kids.

I was raised in a religion where the message about God was skewed. This adversely affected my relationship with God for many years. As an adult, I had a full life as a wife, mom, and nurse, yet, I had an unrequited longing for God. This led me to Chapel Hill Bible Church, where the clarion message of God's love and grace brought me into a dynamic, intimate relationship with Jesus Christ.

About ten years ago, my husband brought our Labrador, Ed home from the pound. Ed was "Bob's dog," but he took daily walks with me. God-thoughts poured into my mind during mine and Ed's time together. Two years ago, Nash, the Labradoodle, came along. He finished off what Ed had started; Nash converted me into an all-out dog lover! Nash is quite a character; he has provided abundant writing material. In my stories, Ed is the "saint," and Nash is usually the "sinner." But my love for both of them is equally intense; as God's kindness has been to me, no matter how far I've strayed.

As science lovers and people of faith, we wanted our children to make up their own minds about God. We desired they "hear the music of faith," as well as "read the notes of reason." (Dr. Francis Collins) We pointed out the evidence for a Creator in the intricate design and fine-tuning of the universe. We gave God due credit as we received divine assistance and saw His positive effects on our character. We provided both information and experience for our children, and that's the goal here for the reader. We hope you will be convinced of the reality of our Good God.

If you have left the faith, I pray my words will make you homesick for God. For the person who's never taken the first step toward God, I hope to stir up curiosity to know Him. I'd be super blessed to reinforce a believer's current faith.

I pray every reader will come into a better understanding of God and enjoy all the amazing privileges of a sweet relationship with Him. He's already built the bridge to you through Jesus. The rest is up to you.

I've never been sorry about loving another dog. And I've, not for one second, regretted walking with our Good God! I only regret not enjoying both earlier.

Living Loved,

Darcey Beale

CHAPTER ONE

Comfort Dog

" ... the God of all comfort, who comforts us in all our troubles ..."
2 Cor. 1:3-4 (NIV)

My daughter's friend pointed out that "Dog" spelled backward spells "God." I'd like to believe this wasn't incidental, that God arranged to share the same alphabet (along with so many of His wonderful attributes) with these sweet canine companions. Dogs are comforting, relational, watchful, forgiving, protective, loyal, patient, consistent, unconditionally-loving, attentive, genuine, etc. — just like their Creator God. God in His kindness designed, created and gifted us with these ambassadors from heaven, who instinctively serve the broken and lead the blind. I believe God smiles when He sees them loving us so well. They ask so little in return, just like their Namesake above.

When I have people over, our Labradoodle, Nash always enjoys everyone. However, recently I had a bunch of friends in, and Nash strangely zoomed in on only one guest. As soon as "Ashley" walked in the door, Nash lost his doggie mind; he skipped the first date and went straight to the proposal! Tall Nash kept wallowing his head into petite Ashley's belly like a love-sick bull smitten with his lady matador.

This reserved young woman didn't know what to do with this shameless, four-legged Romeo. I was mortified and went to put him outside. But she wouldn't have it and assured me he wasn't bothering her. Then, Nash laid down and put his head on her feet! I'd never seen him do this before. He wouldn't budge. He followed her from the table to the den after lunch. Out of all my dinner guests, Nash sensed this one soul really needed some tenderness. While I was too busy cooking, and everyone else was chatting away, Nash noticed the sadness behind her smile and stayed nearby. Later, it dawned on, the ink on Ashley's recent divorce decree was barely even dry.

There's a story in the Bible of a pregnant woman, Hagar, who'd been mistreated, and things became so toxic at home that she ran away to the wilderness. No one cared or came looking for her — except God. She had no food, no water, nor hope that she'd live to see tomorrow, much less to see her child born. But God told Hagar He'd picked out the perfect boy name, which meant she'd be around much longer than this bad day. No doubt, Hagar was filled with the shame that comes with rejection. But God permanently took that away, by promising that her son would be a king — which made her the royal Queen Mom! All it took was for God to see her tears, and His compassion flowed. God hovered near as Provider and Protector to ensure all His good promises to her were fulfilled.[1]

God's word says, *"He's the same today,"* as He was back in Bible times. He still *"rides across the heavens to help us,"* and even now, *"His ears are attentive to our cries."*[2] I know it because He's comforted me more times than I can count. God sends comfort at just the right moment — through His promises, my sweet husband, a friend, a song, etc. And constantly through my two dear comfort dogs.

---

[1] Genesis 16, 21 paraphrase.

[2] Hebrews 13:8; Deuteronomy 33:26; Psalm 34:15 (NIV).

CHAPTER TWO

No More Death Row

"... Jesus has set you free from the law of sin and death." Rom. 8:2 *(NASB)*

My husband called the pound and told them he wanted a Labrador. They called two weeks later and said they had "one" for him. But when he arrived, there were two: a yellow male and a black female for him to pick from. There were no other animals left in the shelter; sadly, every other cat and dog had been euthanized. Bob had a terrible choice to make! He knew the bleak future for the one left behind. Bob made his decision; he came home with *both* dogs.

Bob told me the story, and I assured him it was okay. The kids were thrilled! They quickly named them Bella and Ed. The dogs were welcomed with utmost affection; they were given soft beds to sleep in, and I'm sure they were over fed. We couldn't bear to tie them up but gave them freedom to explore the farm. The next three weeks they were both content, but one day Bella ran away. We did everything you can imagine to find Bella, but sadly, we never did. That was eight years ago, and our dear dog Ed has never strayed.

Ed likes us all, but he adores Bob! He seems to understand Bob rescued him from death row. If Bob is working in the yard, Ed is his shadow. Each evening, Ed lies in the front yard and waits for Bob to return home; you could set your watch by him. Even though he has severe arthritis now, Ed runs down the hill to greet Bob. As soon as the truck tires hit the gravel, Ed takes off like a bullet. Bob stops halfway and puts down the tailgate. He has to pick Ed up these days. As Ed rides back up to the house, he barks the happiest high-pitched sounds. He is so proud to be riding in his beloved Bob's truck bed. Those two have the sweetest relationship.

In a sense, we are all living on death row; ten out of ten people die. As natural as it is, it seems so unnatural. We don't even want to talk about our departure, though it's our number one fear. We will ignore the scary "elephant in the room" until we are forced into a confrontation with it. We hope our own goodness will outweigh the bad and somehow save us. God said there's "no one good, not even one." (Rom 3) That's why He sent His Son. But just as Ed couldn't save himself, and if Bob hadn't shown up, Ed would have been destroyed; so, we cannot do a thing to stop the inevitable up ahead.

Jesus came to rescue us from death, and He does it by offering eternal life. He didn't come to condemn us but wants to forgive every single person. Ray Comfort says, it's like we are all standing at the door of a plane at 10,000 feet getting ready to jump — no wonder we are afraid! We can flap our arms in self-efforts or put on Christ as our metaphorical parachute. When you put your trust in Him completely to make you right with God, His powerful, imperishable life flows into you. The law of gravity (fear and death) no longer has any hold over you.[3] You can really live with abandon when you're saved from your greatest fear!

---

[3] Ray Comfort; www.living waters.com.

CHAPTER THREE

Foster Dog

"A father to the fatherless, a defender of widows, is God in his holy dwelling." Psalm 68:5 (NIV)

Our daughter, Kathryn, rescued Nash, but his incessant barking annoyed the neighbors in her high rise apartment in D.C. Kathryn asked if we could keep him temporarily. (That was two years ago.) Nash was my first experience with an indoor dog. He knocked over trash cans and surfed the counter tops. He is tall, so nothing was safe. We bought an overpriced trash can with a nifty locking lid. We put up baby gates. He could hold his bladder all night, but if we left him alone thirty minutes, he would have accidents. We had to get sitters to go out on a date. We spent a small fortune on obedience classes, vet bills, special food, and carpet cleaning. I was exasperated with this dog and started to resent his being "pushed" upon me.

A few months later, a darling, ten-year-old girl came to live with us. Serenity was a daddy's girl, and no one else would do. Her dad asked us to take her until he could get back on his feet. She cried like her heart would break for the first two nights. I held her in my arms to comfort her. But the real comfort came from Nash. *It was then I fell in love with him.* Nash laid at the foot of Serenity's bed as we read books every night. In the morning, Nash was her prince charming and awakened her with doggie-kisses on her cheeks. He never failed to make her smile and to bring a lovely mood to this little sleepy head. Nash rode to school with her. She was kind of embarrassed when the kids asked who I was, but she proudly introduced Nash as "her dog." They were inseparable. She dressed him up in Bob's neck ties and held tea parties with my fine china on the floor.

About six months into her stay, Serenity's homesickness got the best of her. With tears streaming, she demanded to go home right then and there. I scrambled for words. When I looked at Nash, these thoughts entered my head: I told her that Nash was our temporary foster dog, and that he was only staying until Kathryn came to get him. Serenity said, "Oh! I hope he doesn't leave until after I do." I assured her Kathryn would leave him there for her. Our "fostering Nash" conversation satisfied her.

In retrospect, everything makes perfect sense. God knew we tired, empty nesters needed assistance, and a little girl would need a companion. God is so good like that! He directed all the details with precise timing. We would never have been able to find Nash, but God brought him to us. From a shelter in Indiana to D. C. and then to Kentucky — Nash's journey spanned 1400 miles. When Serenity's dad took her home, Nash and Jesus stayed behind to comfort me. I've never regretted sharing my home with Serenity or Nash; or opening my heart to God.

CHAPTER FOUR

Black-Eyed Susans

"A wife of noble character, who can find? ... she works with eager hands ... She opens her arms to the poor and needy ...." Prov. 31 paraphrase. (NIV)

As I walked with my dogs one hot summer morning, I noticed a small patch of my favorite flowers, Black-Eyed Susans, growing wild. These flowers were Mom's favorite before they were mine. Parkinson's brought Mom's avid gardening to an end a few years ago. My siblings and I went to the florist to order Mom a bunch of her favorite flowers in June of 2013. There wasn't a single Black-Eyed Susan in their stock. So, I ginned up some nerve and went to the lady down the street from my parents' home. I shamelessly asked for a few and told her why. She was thrilled to donate. I thanked her profusely, and with the "Susies" in hand, I returned to the florist and asked her to add them to the arrangement she had already made. The florist was a bit perturbed and told us "they wouldn't hold up, that they were just wildflowers and would look tacky beside the other cultivars." But we insisted — and in the end, those stunning lemon-yellow flowers stood out from the rest, just like Mom's life. This was Mom's last bouquet and was to be placed on top of her casket the next day.

One would notice these lovely brown-eyed beauties in a whole field of other flowers. They tilt their heads upward as if they enjoy the harsh sun; they thrive in August when others are fading away. And that, too, is reminiscent of Mom's indomitable spirit. She selflessly opened her arms and took on daunting responsibility by giving six orphans a home. No doubt, she looked up to the Father for supernatural love and strength. She worked tirelessly and taught us untold life skills, like gardening, canning, cooking, cleaning, and thank-you note writing. As an adult, I'm so grateful, but the most valuable thing she taught me was to believe in God.

Those random perennials in my yard were decorating their little corner of farmland, just as Mom did her part to color her world. Holidays and celebrations were magical as she baked and decorated birthday cakes and put handmade bows atop our gifts. Besides being a wife and homemaker, she was the community nurse, church organist, and Sunday School teacher. She used up everything in her and fulfilled her God-purpose. There was never a dull moment with this dynamic lady; she had a hot temper, but it didn't scare Dad or Jesus away. I expect she is growing her favorite flowers all over heaven and instructing angels how to make pound cakes, a skill I never learned. I've often wondered if Granny Hepler hadn't raised Mom to know Jesus, would Mom have had the compelling love in her heart for six orphans?

CHAPTER FIVE

Ed Keeps Watch

"I am the good shepherd. The good shepherd lays down his life for the sheep." John 10:11(NIV)

My husband brought Ed home from the animal shelter in hopes that he would keep hungry critters away from his garden. Ed has done that and so much more. Even though Ed gets the royal treatment, he is not one bit lazy or spoiled. He's made it his responsibility to protect all of us and every inch of our eighteen acres. He is especially vigilant when night falls, and we hear him chasing coyotes and other invaders away. He has a distinctive scary bark that he uses when his territory is trespassed upon. Many times, Ed has signaled us to come to the garage where we have found him standing over a possum he's just "scared to death." Ed is terrified of storms, but he is a brave heart when he's guarding us. He is better than a doorbell and lets me know as soon as someone turns into our long drive. Knowing Ed is out there watching gives me such peace, especially when Bob's working at night. There are, however, a few times I wish Ed would be a little less scary — like when the UPS guys come. They are not even slightly convinced when I inform them that my sweet doggie wouldn't hurt a flea. I can see why they are skeptical though when I look over at Ed trying his hardest to bite their tires!

🐾 🐾 🐾 🐾
🐾 🐾 🐾 🐾

In Jesus' time, shepherds built sheepfolds out of stacked stones to provide their sheep with shelter from predators in the night. There was an opening in the enclosure, but no door or gate. It wasn't necessary because the shepherd laid his body across the doorway while the sheep slept safely inside. A predator would have to "cross his dead body" to get to the sheep. [4] What beautiful insight this gives us for the kind of relationship King Jesus desires with us. Other kings have their subjects build them castles and stand guard over them — but not Jesus. Our fear of death and judgment is forever put to rest when we come humbly to Him. Just in case we didn't get the picture of the relationship, Jesus lovingly referred to people as sheep in need of a shepherd. He volunteered for the 24/7 job.

Sheep are about the most witless and defenseless animals. They have no fangs, no claws, nor sense of direction. If they fall into a river, their water-logged hair can take them under. They're prone to panic and often injure themselves trying to escape danger. Their well-being is totally dependent on the shepherd. Jesus is the Great Shepherd; He welcomes all to come into the fold. He is the Door. Our trust is the Key. I once ran from Jesus, but now I am blissfully relying on Him completely.

---

[4] Ancient Sheep Fold," Bible History Online; bible-history.com.

CHAPTER SIX

A Bad Moment

"This God—his way is perfect; the word of the LORD proves true; he is a shield for all those who take refuge in him." Psalm 18:30 (ESV)

Nash is a lover boy and people-dog. All our friends and we have fallen in love with him since he came to live here. We can't imagine why anyone would abandon him. Last year, we showed our house to some potential buyers. When the couple arrived, they saw our two dogs and told us they were big dog lovers and had a couple of their own. They immediately started petting our old Lab, Ed. Then the lady went over to Nash, who was temporarily tied up to a line while we showed them the house. Nash was still barking when she reached out to pet him, and his teeth got caught in her long loose bell-sleeves. Nash freaked out, jerked his head back, and his teeth scraped her arm! It all happened so fast; we rushed inside and treated her small abrasion. She was shaken up, and we felt terrible. (Needless to say, we did not sell the house.) I don't blame them if they're convinced Nash is a bad dog.

Skeptics use the handful of Bible scenarios of judgment (after God's multiple warnings) to accuse God of being "mean." Or they point to a poorly behaving Bible character and impugn the Author. The Bible is a true, unedited history book. Just because a story's included in the narrative doesn't mean God approves of bad behavior. (He doesn't.) Granted, there are a few difficult and strange Biblical concepts; however, 99 percent are obviously clear and greatly beneficial. Even so, should our lack of understanding merit a rejection of God? Should one refuse to fly because of a lack of comprehension for how planes stay airborne? For me, it was after having read the entire Bible, that I came to view God as extremely wise and incredibly fair. Since I started putting into practice the precepts therein, my life has only become more fulfilling and stable. *Why would a "mean" God care about our well-being?*

It was logical for me to believe that God is good from just looking at His beneficial laws. There are so many undisputed examples to pick from. For instance, God forbade eating disease causing agents such as rodents, bats, and blood, way back before there was a microscope to reveal the reasons why. (Lev. 11:19, 29; 17:12) God gave the directive to avoid eating animal fats, long before there was an ECG or blood cholesterol lab test. (Lev. 7:23) But we haven't paid attention, and so cardiovascular disease is the number one cause of death globally.[5] Back when the "conventional wisdom" for treating open wounds in ancient Egypt called for poultices using tetanus-laden donkey feces, God's hygienic instructions were to cleanse with fresh running water. (Lev.15) It wasn't until the 1800's that medical science caught up with the Bible and prescribed hand washing and isolation of the sick for preventing the spread of infectious diseases. (Lev. 15)[6] God's wise call to save sexual activity for marriage (Lev. 18) would have protected us from much suffering and prevented the epidemic of terrible debilitating diseases; many cancer causing viruses, infertility from bacterial scarring, and death from overwhelming infections would be unheard of.[7] There would be no need for

---

[5] www.cdc.gov; WHO, World Health Organization, Geneva.

[6] S.I. Mc Millen & David Stern, None of These Diseases, The Bible's Health Secrets for the 21st Century, (Revell, Grand Rapids, 2000).

[7] Health Consequences of STDS; (National Academies Press, US, Washington DC; 1997), nichd.nih.gov;

government financial assistance if we practiced God's commands for helping the orphan, widow, and immigrant. (Deut. 14:29; Lev. 23:22) No rational person could deny the myriad benefits in practicing a weekly day of rest. (Exd. 20:8-11) When we ignore God, He allows consequences and disciplines like any good Father — His patience has limits, but thankfully, His great love is never ending.

CHAPTER SEVEN

Welcome Home, Nash

"God demonstrates His own love for us ... while we were still sinners Christ died for us." Rom. 5:8 (NIV)

When Nash first came to us, he was used to city life in D.C., being cooped up indoors or walking outside on a leash. But after coming to Kentucky, he had seventeen acres of green grass calling him outside. Nash loved looking out and left smudges on every single window we have. Our sons, Chu and Young-min, agreed wholeheartedly with Nash that it was much nicer outdoors. They also came to our farm in Kentucky after being accustomed to urban life in Seoul. Their favorite place to be was on the porch snapping pictures of unobstructed sunsets and staring at the brilliant stars and fireflies. I often heard them say, "Wow, God!"

Nash longed to be outside, and anytime a door was opened, he tried to make his escape. One afternoon, he succeeded and ran under the neighbor's fence. I was frantic and wondered if he'd find his way back home. I yelled until I was out of breath. Old Ed was standing quietly beside me the whole time, then suddenly, he joined in with a high-pitched bark. It was the exact one he reserves for when my husband's gray truck shows up at the end of the workday.

Now, Ed had been king at our house for twelve years until Nash moved in last week. Nash was the new "darling doggie" hogging all the attention. He was allowed to stay inside with us while Ed remained outside. Ed's barking was effective — Nash came running home! My prior exasperation disappeared, and I was filled with relief. There was no jealousy from Ed. He and Nash jumped and bumped into each other like two victorious athletes.

Jesus sometimes told parables that were difficult to understand. But this one was blatantly about God's radical unmerited love.

The story began with a kind father giving an entitled son a generous inheritance. (Luke 15) The son moved to another country and partied his dad's money away. As a last resort, he headed home. Surprisingly, the father ran and embraced him like he was a returning war hero and made plans for a huge celebration. The father robed his son's frail, dirty body — just as God does when He forgives a returning sinner and clothes them in His Son's perfection. The father slipped the family ring back onto his son's finger — to represent how Father-God adopts the repentant sinner into His family and gives them an inheritance. He put new shoes on his son's bare feet for dancing at the party — just as a God-life fills us with joy and many reasons to cut a rug.

The older brother had been working hard all of his life to impress his father, and now he resented all the mercy being given to his rebel brother. He severely lacked an understanding of the father's heart. I have been both of these guys, but I repented of my misinformed, cold thoughts toward God; His love is freely given to the one who comes near through Jesus. Friend, all you have to do is come close to this good Father-God! Get ready to be forgiven of every sin and treated as if it never happened. Being in a love-relationship with this God is a beautiful celebration that never ends.

CHAPTER EIGHT

A Bark in the Night

"My sheep hear my voice, I know them, and they follow me." John 10:27 (KJV)

I opened my eyes upon being awakened in the middle of the night by raucous barking outside. I tiptoed in the dark and followed the sound to a window near where Nash was sitting on the porch. I tapped gently on the window without saying a word. Nash ran over excitedly to peer inside, only to be confronted with my dark silhouette staring back at him. He sprang back like he'd been stung, bared his teeth, and started growling at me. He thought I was an intruder who'd somehow sneaked by him. I didn't want to awaken my husband, so I whispered, "Nash! It's me!" He heard and recognized my voice, and that made all the difference. All hackles disappeared; Nash pressed his cute nose to the window and did his friendliest tail-wag. I'm sure he was wondering, "Is it time for breakfast yet?"

When Adam and Eve refused to listen to God, their spirits died that day. Every person since then inherited dead spirits that are unable to hear God's voice until their spirits are born again. (Rom. 5:12) Mercifully, God gave us a conscience to protect us from complete self-destruction. However, it's a temporary imperfect fix, because when we go against our conscience, it becomes dull. Eventually, we aren't bothered by our own sin and selfishness. This mindset destroys our relationships and eventually ruins our lives. We cannot help hurting others; unfortunately, it is exactly what comes natural for us.

When we give ourselves to God, He resurrects our spirits and puts His love and Holy Spirit inside. (1 Pet. 1:3) God's Spirit then provides strength to love people as Jesus did. You'll know the Spirit's in there when you start changing from a lover of self, to a lover of God and others. As we experience the resultant blessings in our families and friendships, we'll be more apt to believe what God says and put it into practice. Born-again believers cannot ignore the Spirit's dynamic voice in the way we did our consciences. (Rom. 8:14)

After Jesus resurrected and went to heaven, He poured out His Spirit on His small band of followers. These fearful men and women were instantly transformed! Peter, who had denied even knowing Jesus, started fearlessly speaking about Him to huge crowds. (Acts 2) Paul went from being a hater of Jesus, to being a tireless preacher, author, and missionary for Him. (Acts 9) They both literally gave their lives for the cause. The movement flourished as God spoke through the Spirit and enabled His believers to hear and obey His instructions. He gave them power to love their neighbors sacrificially in the worst of times. Christianity spread, and in 380 A.D., the once hostile Roman Empire was converted without a fight; God's love was their only weapon, and that was all it took.[8]

---

[8] Roman Emperor Constantine's Conversion to Christianity; classicehistory.net; January 14, 2020.

CHAPTER NINE

Don't Die Before Your Time

"Be not overly wicked and do not be a fool -- why die before your time?"
Ecc. 7:17 (NIV)

Ed has always stayed nearby when we are out walking. If Bob is with us, Ed is his little shadow. But Nash had to go through doggie-obedience classes to be able to walk off-leash. He was doing so well until this morning. We were around thirty feet from the end of our drive and about to turn toward home, when both dogs noticed something and began barking furiously. I looked up to see a jogger across the highway. It all happened in a split second; Nash took off like a bullet. I screamed hysterically but may as well have saved my breath. I couldn't do a thing and just said, "Lord help!"

The jogger saw what was transpiring, he stopped and turned toward Nash. He waved his arms menacingly and bellowed, "Go home! Go home!"

Nash abruptly stopped and stared at the "big scary man." My heart was in my throat as Nash turned toward me and ran back into my awaiting arms. That little incident probably scared five years off my life. Nash went back on-leash for a while after that.

🐾 🐾 🐾 🐾

There's unavoidable suffering because we live in a sin-sick world, but keeping God's laws protects us from so much harm. God created us, so He knows what works best to prolong and enhance our lives. God didn't usually give the reason for His commands; however, time and technology have given us much insight into His wisdom. Perhaps God was thinking of the terrible conditions that would plague crowded cities, like poverty, disease, and violent crime[9] when He said "fill the land" or in other words, spread out. [10] When God said, "not to eat the fat of the meat,"[11] He didn't offer an explanation of the risk of cardiovascular disease — the number one cause of death globally.[12] Without providing a rationale, God prohibited sex outside marriage. If ever there was wisdom in adhering to "a pound of prevention," this would be the thing, and deadly sexually-transmitted diseases would not be epidemic.

Respecting and reverencing God means to take His words seriously, as one would a trusted boss or wise king. Healthy fear of God is like a guardrail that keeps us from falling over a cliff. God's laws protect us and maximize our ability to thrive. God has a plan to give us a set number of days on earth before we are even born. (Psa.139:16) There is an expiration date for our life here. God gives us all the information we need to finish well and not leave a moment too soon.

---

[9] "Urban Crime -- Are Crime Rates Higher in Urban Areas?" On-line Law Library; law.jrank.org. Web solutions LLC, 2020.

[10] Gen. ch. 1:28, 9:1, 11:8-9.

[11] Lev. ch. 7:23-24.

[12] Fast Stats-Deaths and Mortality; www.cdc.gov.

CHAPTER TEN

Blue Water

"Pure and genuine religion in the sight of God the Father means caring for orphans and widows in their distress ... " James 1:27 (NIV)

Nash had a terrible case of the "runs" and had to visit the vet. His appetite was improving, but his water bowl remained untouched. So, I resorted to what I did when my kids were sick. I gave him a popular blue sports drink. I wondered if Nash would even notice the blue "water" in his bowl. I filled his dish and stepped back. Nash slowly walked over. Surprisingly, he took a sip. That led to another, and then he quickly slurped up every drop. It would have made for a perfect T.V. commercial. He laid back down, and I refilled his bowl in case he wanted more. Then old Ed walked up, and Nash leaped up and ran over to protect his "liquid assets." He seemed to glare at Ed and added a low bass growl. If Nash only realized I was willing to run to the store for more, maybe he would have shared.

🐾 🐾 🐾 🐾
🐾 🐾 🐾 🐾

God is a generous giver, and He calls His followers to show His compassion by assisting the poor. He commanded farmers to leave behind free produce for the needy. (Lev. 23:22) He set a year for the rich to return land to its original owner (without charge) and to emancipate indentured servants (regardless if they'd paid their debt). (Lev 25) This ancient Law of Jubilee was considered so extreme and "inconvenient" that it was most often ignored and interpreted as "ideological."

After Christ came and filled believers with His Spirit and amazing love, things changed dramatically. He set the tone and the pattern to "give till it hurts." The Spirit still enables Christ followers to do hard things for the good of humanity. There have been untold acts of great benevolence by His followers throughout the centuries since.

One great example of a man with God's heart, George Muller, started 117 schools for poor children and housed over 10,000 orphans in his lifetime. He took his financial needs directly to God and journaled over 50,000 answers to prayer. At one point, the orphanage was completely out of food, but George sat at the table with the orphans and bowed his head and gave thanks anyways. When he said "Amen," there was a knock at the door. Two trucks carrying bread and milk had broken down outside. (You know how this story ends.)[13]

There are 2,752 Pregnancy Care Centers across the U.S. that provide over two million women with around $161 million in free material support annually.[14] Years ago, I was so touched when my son, Jeremy, used his birthday money to purchase an infant car seat for a needy client of our local PCC.

Samaritan's Purse donated twenty tons of supplies to help fight Covid-19 in Italy, including a field hospital with ventilators and staff. They did the same in NYC.[15] Eight Days of Hope started in response to Hurricane Katrina, and their army of volunteers have

---

[13] George Muller: Man of Faith, by Basil Miller; (Bethany House Publishers, Minneapolis MN 55438; 1972), p.33, 52, 65.

[14] Charlotte Lozier Institute, 2017; 2800 Shirlington Rd. Suite 1200, Arlington VA 22206.

[15] Samaritan's Purse International, 2020; Boone NC 28607.

deployed for sixty natural disasters statewide since.[16] Joni Tada, a quadriplegic herself, has donated over 170,000 wheelchairs to the disabled poor across the globe.[17] These are just a tiny sampling of people who live out their faith by sharing their resources. They can because they know God will provide whatever they need, because he always has.

---

[16] Spectrum News, May 9, 2020.

[17] Charity Navigator, 2019.

CHAPTER ELEVEN

A Dog's Purpose

"For I know the plans I have for you," declares the Lord ..." Jer. 29:11 (NIV)

Nash and Ed seem to love fulfilling their dog-assignments, which are to: scare off strangers, greet our friends, and keep critters out of Bob's garden. The dogs get a little over-zealous in intimidating the mailman and UPS guys. They seem to be most upset about strange trucks being in our driveway; they appear to be trying to bite their tires. Otherwise, the dogs love company as much as Bob and I do.

Nash and Ed especially love Mickey and Lucia, who dog and house-sit for us. I'm pretty sure they spoil our pets royally while we are gone. When we return, our dogs have newly acquired habits of barging inside and must be reoriented to their purpose and to residing outside.

God created all of us for a specific purpose and designed us perfectly for this plan. Knowing the reason for our existence motivates us to get up in the morning and to give our best. God did not create anyone to just take up space but desires that we contribute something valuable to the world. He puts God-sized dreams into our hearts in hopes that we will turn to Him for help in accomplishing them. Doing this one thing well will give us deep satisfaction and bring God praise.

God made us as three-part beings: body, spirit, and soul. When all three parts are functioning well, we are better able to carry out His good work in the world. (1 Thes.5:23) Our soul is who we are, it's from our souls that we make our decisions. Our souls are either led by our spirit or driven by the body's cravings. When our spirits are alive (born again), we are tuned-in to God and able to receive His vital graces of love, wisdom, and self-control — things that ensure our well-being and success. When our spirits are dead, our souls are prone to being enslaved to whatever the body craves. This is often how we end up with destructive habits and addictions.

God gave us a perfect world, but people brought disease and death into it — not Him. Like a child holding a burst balloon, we're angry at "Dad" who inflated it and gave it to us. We ruined it, because we ignored his instructions on how to keep it whole. [18] People reject God's voice of reason, then blame Him for the painful fallout. God loved us too much to make us robots. True freedom requires God to give us a choice of good versus evil. We can choose to rebel against God's good plan, but the consequences are written in stone. Sin always destroys something — relationships, finances, our health, the environment, etc. The ensuing chaos keeps us busy and prevents us from completing our God-assignment. But the good news is, God sent us His Son to give us a new spirit and a fresh start. It only takes a humble heart and faith that Jesus is completely adequate to clean up our mess and a child-like trust that allows Him to be King over us.

---

[18] "God our Father,"20/20 Vision Series, by Kory Cunningham, hardin baptist.org., 3/8/20.

CHAPTER TWELVE

Hungry Dog

"Taste and see that the Lord is good ..." Psalm 34:8 (NIV)

Nash came to us with severe stomach issues, along with picky taste buds. I lost track, but we must have tried ten different foods. It would take him all day to eat one bowl, and everything gave him the runs. We resorted to making his food and found such satisfaction in watching him gobble it up and his weight improve. Initially, his stomach calmed down, but eventually, his troubles returned. A breeder recommended a variety with sweet potatoes and salmon. The first time we served the new stuff, Nash stared down at his bowl like he was depressed. I can't say I blamed him, it had a strong fishy odor and looked completely different. Eventually, his hunger drove him to take one nibble, which led to another until it was gone. He loves it now, and his tummy does as well.

🐾 🐾 🐾 🐾
🐾 🐾 🐾 🐾

I was adopted at age five by a wonderful Christian couple. I am sure they saved my life. Mom diligently planted huge gardens, cooked wonderful meals, and taught us life skills. Dad worked overtime to provide for our household of nine on a blue-collar salary. He had a long fuse, but when he got angry, it could be scary. He was a man of few words and was unable to communicate the affirmation I craved. I assumed (wrongly) that he and God were very disappointed with me.

We belonged to a separatist church sect that read the Bible through cloudy glasses. They taught that salvation was free, but you had to be perfect to keep it. I sought God with all my heart and dutifully wore long dresses, but never had any lasting peace. After college, I moved away from home and fell apart; chasing male attention became my new religion.

Bob and I dated three years and got engaged between breakups. I carried a ton of insecurity into our eventual marriage. We were spiritually dead and broken. By God's grace, we attended Chapel Hill Bible Church where we heard the full gospel straight from the scriptures. The pastor addressed us all as "*friends*," then reassured us that *God loves us and accepts us on the basis of Jesus' perfect life.* He said that *salvation is a secure gift, an unbreakable covenant, an adoption by God.* (Eph.1:5-9) Relief and pure love washed over me. For so many years I struggled, but in that instant, I knew I was accepted by God. I've never been the same.

Over the past twenty-nine years, God's been ridding me of insecurity and other toxic things. He's given both my husband and I an insatiable appetite for the Bible that has been transforming our minds and character. God daily straightened the path before us, and His love flowed into us. No doubt, He saved our marriage and healed all our relationships — including the one with Dad. God gave us a sweet life of purpose and a bunch of darling kids to raise. I'm so glad I didn't give up searching for the truth, and that I took another taste of our good God!

CHAPTER THIRTEEN

Goodbye, Sweet Marie

Jesus said, "And if I go and prepare a place for you, I will come back and take you to be with me that you also may be where I am." John 14:3 (NIV)

Marie was our beloved cat for nine years. Sweet Marie had a timid, reclusive personality. So, we didn't think anything of it when we didn't see her for a day or two. I happened to go out to the storage barn for something late in the afternoon on Monday and found Marie sleeping on the cool concrete. I picked her up and was shocked at how light she was. I noticed she seemed a little thin last week, so I gave her a dose of worm medicine. She continued to eat. But this was a dramatic, ominous drop overnight. The vet would be closing by the time I got there today. I knew she would be put in a kennel for the night, and that would stress her out. We planned to take her first thing tomorrow.

I took her inside and held her on my lap and stroked her soft velvet fur. When I set out her favorite canned cat food, she was able to eat some, but she refused any fluids. She was an outdoor cat and always skittish about being inside. She headed toward the door, and I let her go.

The next day I couldn't find her and started to really worry. Bob found her lifeless body Wednesday morning (9/12/19). It was so hard to say goodbye to our sweet Marie. As I called all our adult kids to tell them of Marie's passing, they each expressed tender memories and their sadness at her dying too soon. When you love someone, the parting will always be "too soon."

Adam and Eve rebelled against God, and as a consequence, death comes to all of creation. It is so sad that innocent animals would now have such brief lives. Likewise, Jesus died in the prime of His life. Even though He was sinless, He paid the penalty for the whole world's sins. The Father and Son planned it out of their great love for us. Jesus' selfless act removed the sting of death for all who will just turn away from sin and believe in Him. He has promised them unending life after death.

I've read and heard many fascinating accounts of believers who were clinically dead and then revived. Their descriptions were consistent: death lasted a split second while their soul flew upward. Jesus welcomed and enveloped them in His love. Clothing was woven out of light! Introductions were made to loved ones never met before. And they saw many animals there in heaven.

An event occurred that reinforced my belief in life after death. It was when my own dear Mom lay motionless and comatose for several days before her last breath. My siblings and I were gathered around her, and Dad was sitting at the left of her bed. Just before Mom passed, I saw her raise her left hand and wave goodbye to Dad. He reached out and took her hand.

God's concern for all His creatures is indisputable in the account of Noah's ark. God engineered a huge boat, one and a half football fields long and seven stories high, knowing that only Noah's small family of eight would embark. I believe we can look forward to being reunited with our pets in heaven, because God is extravagant and kind like that.

CHAPTER FOURTEEN

Nash Loves What We Hate

"... though your sins are like scarlet they will be white as snow ..."Isa. 1:18 (NIV)

When we first allowed Nash to be an outdoor dog with his buddy Ed, his new freedom kept him happy as a clam at high tide. But the hot, humid days of summer diminished the novelty of it right away. We'd love for him to come back inside, except he now frequently has vile brown matter stuck to his fur. Rotting deer carcasses and cow manure are two of Nash's favorite things ... he rolls around in them! Since Nash cannot clean himself, we take the initiative and do all the dirty work. We head to Tractor Supply and gladly pay the small fee to use their awesome doggie-wash station. They provide towels, shampoo, a dog-sized tub, and blow dryer. Nash absolutely hates it, but we adore the results. He comes out smelling like orange blossoms without a trace of his old smelly self. After he is dry and combed, his fur is so beautiful, fluffy, and blond — we can't keep our hands off him. His reward is being allowed back inside to snuggle with us on the couch.

God loves us so much and wants us to be near. But our sin greatly repels Him. God is pure love; He can't stand to watch as our selfishness ruins our relationships and wrecks our lives. God knows we are helpless to change or to clean up our act. So, He took the initiative and provided everything necessary for a spiritual bath. Jesus' blood washes away all sin. He paid the price with His own life, so all who are willing can have an intimate relationship with God. You don't need to try to "get yourself straightened up" before coming to God. None of us can anyway. God's very pleased with humble folks who admit they need cleansing and trust Jesus to do it all for them.

There's no sin too bad that God won't forgive either, nor any habit too ingrained that His power cannot change. The good news comes after the bad news. We cannot earn a right standing with God — it's a gift — based not on our own goodness, but on the Son's perfect life. The defining word for this is *grace*. Grace is God not giving us the punishment we deserve. Grace is Him giving us the good things we did not earn. Grace is God saving us and securing our relationship with Him forever. Grace is God continuing to save us every day by another great gift — the Holy Spirit.

God's Spirit draws believers into the Bible, and the words transform our thoughts. Sin that used to be irresistible will become repulsive; you'll hit your knees and ask God to remove it from your soul. No need to be discouraged when you fail to live up to His standards. Jesus already did. You are a child of God's forever, so get back up and start walking with your Father again. Peter denied even knowing Jesus, right when Jesus needed him most. Jesus took the initiative to restore the relationship. Instead of a reprimand, Jesus gave Peter a clean slate and promoted him to leader of the church! Jesus trusted Peter with this huge responsibility because His own Spirit would be inside Peter empowering and leading him every step of the way.

CHAPTER FIFTEEN

Forgive Quickly

"Even if they sin against you seven times in a day and seven times come back to you saying, 'I repent,' you must forgive them." Luke 17:4 (NIV)

It was drizzling only slightly as the dogs and I set out this morning. They ran ahead of me with enthusiasm, completely undeterred by the weather. I was surprised about Ed choosing to join us. He is deathly afraid of storms and huddles in the garage long before the first raindrop. I was hoping to beat the rain and get in at least one lap. About halfway down the hill, the gentle drizzle turned into a pelting rain. I did an about-face and started jogging home. Ed immediately followed me. I paused and called Nash who had run out ahead. He turned and seemed to look at us with such disappointment. His eyes were pleading, "Oh come on … it's just a little rain."

I started thinking about the day last week when Nash couldn't be begged or bribed to go walk. He was too busy chewing a nasty old bone. Now the tables were turned, and he was begging me to walk with him. I wimped out and ran toward the dry house. Nash finally decided to follow suit. He beat Ed and me to the top of the hill and welcomed us like he hadn't seen us in days! (Only people pout.)

When Jesus' friends asked Him how many times they were required to forgive an offender, He basically responded, "Forgive quickly and as often as necessary." Jesus and the Father do this for us. Thankfully, God has put no limits on how many times He will forgive us; plus, there's no sin too bad. In Bible days, God forgave

King David for murder and adultery. He's forgiven me more times than I can count. When God removes guilt by taking away your sin, it leaves you so filled with His love that it will automatically spill over to everyone — even your enemies. No other religion espouses love and forgiveness like Christianity.

God sent His Son to make peace between Himself and sinners. He knows we all need forgiveness on a daily basis, and He offers it to us. God desires that we treat others the way that He treats us. He wants us to express love by valuing and maintaining our relationships — that's accomplished largely by offering constant forgiveness. Forgiveness is such a high priority with God that He warned if we don't offer it to others, He will withhold it from us. He knew we'd need a severe penalty to deter us from nursing grudges and building high walls of bitterness around our hearts. God doesn't want us to live in isolation and created us to enjoy many meaningful relationships. Friend, what does this tell you about the heart of God?

CHAPTER SIXTEEN

Bad Hair Days

"See what great love the Father has lavished on us ..." 1 John 3:1 (NIV)

I thoroughly appreciate my two dogs and how they greet me every morning like I'm Mrs. Beauty Queen, no matter if I have a bedhead or funky breath. I know it's silly, but all this unconditional doggie-love really touches me. Last year, I transitioned to gray hair, and for months, I looked like a bizarre hybrid skunk lady. It was embarrassing to realize, at age fifty-five, I'm still self-conscious about my hair. I believe it's normal to fret a bit over our hair; it's even addressed in the Bible — *that God gave us our hair as our crown and glory.* (1 Cor. 11:15)

I think my daughters are beautiful, but they can't see it themselves. They don't trust my opinion because they don't think I can be unbiased (probably not). My youngest daughter shares my (formerly) brown, curly hair gene. I always hated my curls — but I absolutely love it on her! I never knew what to do with my own — however, I found it easy to style all of theirs. When my girls called themselves ugly, I quickly responded, "God doesn't make junk!"

While I was preaching to them, I started believing it for myself. Undoubtedly, it helped my insecurity to have a sweet husband loving me for almost thirty years. But it's truly been God's love that has transformed me. When we come to understand how loved we are by the God of the universe, it makes all the difference in the world. Then we have enough love to share as we follow Jesus' lead.

There's a Bible story of a woman who noticed Jesus' dusty feet. (Luke 7) She used her tears and lovely hair to clean away the dirt! In essence, she gave her "crown and glory" back to her King. In a room crowded with disapproving men, her courage was brazen. I'm sure the women back then were just as concerned about their hair. (There'd be no quick shower for shampooing either.) She must have had a tender encounter with Jesus, which compelled her to reciprocate with an audacious act of her own. After she finished, His feet were spotless, but it wasn't enough. She then covered them with kisses and drenched them with expensive perfume. This unnamed woman demonstrated true love with an intentional act that God honored on the pages of Scripture for all time.

Another intentional act involving feet that I'll never forget, was when my daughter, Kathryn, was on mission in Mexico. She took off her flip-flops and gave them to a barefoot pregnant teenager — then walked around barefoot on trash strewn soil for the rest of that day. But, the ultimate intentional act of love was when Jesus took off His golden crown and exchanged it for a cruel crown of thorns. God blesses every person with rain and sunshine, and many other good things, but those who wholeheartedly give themselves to Jesus receive salvation and a special kind of favor.

CHAPTER SEVENTEEN

Nash Trusts Me

"And without faith it is impossible to please God, because anyone who comes to him must believe that he exists and he rewards those who earnestly seek him." Heb. 11:6 (NIV)

Nash is really smart for a doggie. I shouldn't brag, but I think he can even tell time. He may be out roaming the farm, but when it's time for supper, he starts home. He is able to deduce that we fed him yesterday and believes we will today. Even when he cannot see us inside, he logically comes near to the place he knows we generally are. Nash gets in his old wing back chair on the porch just outside my den. My sweet doggie stays calm and waits patiently. Nash's peaceful demeanor and close proximity reveal he trusts in us. And we always reward him for believing in us and for coming near — by filling his bowl with something good.

In response to the question "Why doesn't God just show Himself?" Ravi Zacharias told a parable of a king whose son fell in love with a commoner. The king advised his son to take on the appearance of a poor man to ensure her love was genuine and not swayed by his royal status.[19] Jesus is our Peasant-Prince. He is God in human flesh who came down from heaven to win our hearts. A dirty, drafty stable was his delivery room; a feeding trough His makeshift crib. He grew up as Joseph's son with lots of innuendo, so when He disclosed His true identity, people mocked. This would be understandable, if it weren't for His public miracles

---

[19] Ravi Zacharias; rzim.org.

35

and a sinless life of sacrifice lived before their eyes. His resurrection cinched His God-status for His followers. But even that still was not enough evidence for His detractors. Maybe it was that Jesus assimilated so well as a humble man, people found it hard to believe in His deity?

It requires some faith to believe in an unseen God. The Bible declares that there is plenty of proof in nature. (Rom.1:18-22) Scientists agree that the universe is extremely complex and so finely tuned, that it seems as if it were being directed. How can it be logical to believe in a driverless, celestial Indy 500, where planets spin and simultaneously orbit the sun without a single collision for millennia?

Hubble's discovery of the expanding universe, along with the amazing structure of nature, compelled Einstein to acknowledge a divine hand (though he wasn't religious). Now science had to admit there was an instant beginning without any existing materials. This goes right along with the record in Genesis.

Technology unveils handiwork like that of an intelligent Designer; microscopes reveal complicated cellular factories and miles of intricate DNA patterns. There are so many critical constants that would seem to require a Manager; if earth's tilt, gravity, or oxygen levels were only minutely altered, life wouldn't be possible. It goes against logic to doubt the objective evidence in support of faith in a Creator-God.

CHAPTER EIGHTEEN

Jumping Cat

"For it is by grace you have been saved, through faith - not from yourselves, it is the gift of God." Eph. 2:8 (NIV)

We went to the Humane Society and came home with another gray Tabby. Our daughter, Song named her "Nabi" which means "kitten" or "butterfly" in Korean. Nabi's temporary home was our screened back porch until she was acclimated to her new address. Poor lonely Nabi begged to come inside, but we are allergic, so that wouldn't work. She constantly hopped up and down on her hind legs while frantically tapping at the French door. Perhaps she hoped all this activity would help her scale the door. It was downright pitiful to watch all her futile efforts and seeing her wear herself out. She was expertly fitted for climbing trees, but everything about her cat-anatomy worked against her for ascending slippery glass. Even if she could somehow propel herself three feet upwards, turning the knob would be impossible for her tiny fingerless paws. I felt so sorry for her that I stopped quite often to go out there to play. What was impossible for Nabi was easy for me. Doorknobs and doors were made by humans to be opened by us — not by critters or cats.

God gave His people 613 laws as a "mirror," to show them they were sinners in need of a Savior. Laws and mirrors weren't meant to wash away dirt. We religious people try to do the impossible and keep the rules in an attempt to earn God's approval. We pile up good deeds but are never assured we've done enough. It's impossible to obey them all, so we zero in on a few rules that are easier to keep. My childhood tradition focused primarily on women's apparel and adornment.[20] Upon being asked about which rule was most important, Jesus didn't say baptism or church attendance. It wasn't as easy as being modest. He obliterated any self-efforts for being righteous, and said, *"Love God and people (perfectly) as I have loved you."* (John 13:34) If that weren't unreachable enough, He raised the bar higher, *"If you break one law, you're guilty of all ... if you think about committing a sin, it's counted against you."* (James 2:10) Then finally, *"Love your enemies."* (Matt.5:44)

God's impossible standards were meant to force us to cry, "Uncle" — to quit trying and start trusting Him. God knew if we could save ourselves independent of Him, we would. His laws are our "glass door"; that's why Jesus came down. What's impossible for us, Jesus has already done. His righteousness will be credited to our account when we turn to Him. (Rom.4:25; 2Cor.5:21) God planned all along to make us holy and give us eternal life. (Eph.1:4) When we trust fully that what Jesus did on the cross was more than adequate to pay for every sin, we are, spiritually speaking, *"raised to new life, made holy and clothed with Christ."* (Gal.3:27) Ever after, when God sees us, it's with the same love and acceptance He has for His Son. (1John3:1)

---

[20] Outward Holiness (Wesleyan Holiness Church standards of conduct and dress) Wikipedia.

CHAPTER NINETEEN

Nash's Stains

"But if we walk in the light as he is in the light we have fellowship with one another, and the blood of Jesus His Son purifies us from all sin."
1 John 1:7 (NIV)

If I may be real here, Nash has peed, pooped, or thrown up all over our house. Nash can go all night without an accident, yet if I leave him alone inside for fifteen minutes, he does. Now when I go upstairs, I must walk past two basketball-sized stains on my floor. We have paid two different cleaning services only to see a faint stain reappear after the carpet has dried. I'm so thankful for my wooden floors downstairs. All it takes to remove all stains and odors is a bucket of hot soapy water and a willing soul. So, I finally waved the white flag and drilled eight holes in my staircase and hung a doggie-gate between Nash and the carpeted floors upstairs.

Sometimes I ask myself why I'm willing to dole out cash for carpet cleaning, having ugly stains on my rugs, or the extra work of washing sofa cushions? The only answer is that my love for Nash overrides everything this messy, aggravating dog does. I wouldn't even want to imagine life without him! Nash has become part of our family. Obviously, Nash is a royal mess-maker, and he cannot clean up after himself. I realize if we're going to have him around, we must be willing to accept a few stinky chores and incur expenses.

God created us and loves us dearly. He wants us near Him. But He is holy, and sin repulses Him. Ever since Adam sinned, we're all born rebels; we love our sin more. God sees the big picture: how sin spreads like a demonic plague through households and destroys whole nations like an atomic bomb. Therefore, the punishment had to be severe; the consequence or "wages" or due penalty for sin is death. God is a righteous Judge, so He must uphold the law and give the sentence. We're helpless to change ourselves or our destiny of eternal death and separation from holy God.

But God the Father and the Son made a plan of mercy long before the first human sinned. The escape route would involve some wood, so God planted a seedling for a tree. God watered and watched it grow tall, years before it was felled and sawn into boards. He put the iron ore into the ground that would be melted into a hammer and spikes. Arrangements were made for Jesus to be our surrogate to take our guilty verdict and death penalty. He was nailed to a wooden cross for the sins of the world. It's almost too good to be true, but those who simply trust Jesus as their Savior are forgiven of every sin — past, present and future! They never have to fear death or judgment again. Even though we still struggle with temptation, now God sees us as saints. He adopts us as sons and daughters forever. When we sin, the Holy Spirit gently reminds us we are saints and children of the King. He'll empower us to be sincerely sorry and to move on without any shame. When we get to heaven, all our bent to sinning will completely vanish. There will be no more sin, guilt, or shame for Jesus to wipe away. I'll probably celebrate this fact for the first ten thousand years!

CHAPTER TWENTY

Don't Take Your Dog for Granted

"Give thanks always and for everything to God the Father in the name of our Lord Jesus Christ." Eph. 5:20 (ESV)

We were going out of town the next day and arranged for our friends, Mickey and Lucia, to keep Nash (still an indoor dog then) and Serenity for the weekend. Mickey picked Nash up Thursday evening and planned to get Serenity after school on Friday. He would stop by our house and feed our other pets each day on his way home from work. We had the best laid plan, except we never anticipated how terribly we'd miss Nash during our short separation.

Thursday evening's story time was restless without Nash at the foot of Serenity's bed. Mine and Bob's breakfast on Friday was strange with no Nash begging for food. But Nash's absence was most painfully evident when it came time to awaken Serenity for school! Everything was difficult without him here to sweeten her morning mood with his doggie-kisses. Our girl completely unraveled when Nash wasn't along for the *one-mile ride to school.* By eight a.m. Nash was sorely missed in a jillion ways. Later, my morning walk with Ed lacked the typical excitement minus our bouncy Labradoodle. Not having Nash revealed how much joy he adds to our daily life. Now I felt awful for complaining about the few extra chores he caused. His little messes and improprieties now seemed just that — *little.*

The sad fact is the people I claim to love the most, I often take for granted. For years, I didn't make the same effort in thanking my husband, as I would a friend, for all the ways he blesses me. The antidote to this destructive mindset is all over the Bible! God's ways should be "common sense," but they are not commonly practiced. What would our relationships look like if we habitually had a grateful attitude, verbally acknowledged our loved one's every act of kindness, or penned a "Thank you" note for every gift? What if we were like Jesus and raced to be first to serve and to forgive?!

God is wise and kind; He designed families and relationships and knows how they function best. God knew that no one could thrive in a place where toxic, demanding, ungrateful attitudes are prevalent. This is why He gave us the admonitions like, "Be thankful always and for everything" and "Love as I have loved you." No exceptions. God didn't define love as a feeling, but as an action; its synonym is patience. (1Cor.13:4) It is hard work; but it works. Love is worth it and leaves no regrets. When I consistently offer the same kindness to my loved ones that I'd give to a stranger at the door, our house becomes a sanctuary. I've found that it's only when I start my day with God-time that a good attitude is even possible. And God grants me wisdom to appreciate my blessings while I still have them.

CHAPTER TWENTY-ONE

Pet Names and Nicknames

"To the one who is victorious ... I will give that person a white stone with a new name written on it, known only to the one who receives it."
Rev. 2:17 (NIV)

We rescued our dogs when they were adult dogs. Our kids have named all our pets. It was uncanny how their new names perfectly suited their dog-personalities. Our kids took Ed's name from Edward, the handsome, good-natured vampire from the Twilight series. We also think Ed is handsome in his golden coat, plus he is extremely good-natured (unless you are a possum or the UPS guy). Our youngest daughter, Kathryn, rescued Nash and named him after Nashville, where she attended college.

I've chosen a couple of pet names for Ed and Nash. When Ed is struggling to keep up, now that he is so arthritic, I often encourage him with, "Come on Eddie-Boy! You can make it!" Fun Nash gets the silly title of "Noodle Doodle." I am so shamelessly silly over these dear dogs. I talk to them like they are my children. I used to roll my eyes at dog-people like me, not too long ago.

God loves us and pursues us with everything at His disposal. He wants to save us from our destructive ways and adopt us as His own children. Then He gives us a life of purpose and honor with new identities. God calls repentant sinners, "Saints." Followers of Jesus are given the title "Christian"; which means "little Christ." Jesus will bestow a special name on us when we get to heaven that only He will use — like a nickname spoken between two BFF's. (Rev. 2:17)

Jesus had many names: Lord, King, Healer, Teacher, God, Emanuel, Savior, Messiah, etc. My favorite is "Jesus." That name is powerful and not just a sequence of letters. God promises that *one day every knee will bow at Jesus' Name.* (Phil.2:10-11) God's promises that our prayers will get special attention when we end them *"In Jesus' Name."* (John 16:23-24) When God's children reverently say **Jesus** — the Name He loves above all others — God goes to work on their behalf!

I met a most pitiful man living in a dump in Mexico, named Cephas. The Mexican children made fun of him and called him "crazy drunk." Cephas came to our mission team's work site to beg; he was filthy and drunk. I felt God tell my spirit that He wanted me to reach out to him. I read Jeremiah 29:11 from the Bible, then told him through an interpreter how much God loved him and had a much better plan for his life; I prayed for him in Jesus' Name. Afterwards, Cephas fell to his knees and wept and prayed in Spanish — I recognized Jesús Christo! He rose up a radically changed man — praising God and completely clear headed! Cephas went home, came back in clean clothes, and shaven. None of the local Mexicans had ever seen him sober. We heard later that Cephas-the-Saint was traveling around Mexico telling others the power of Jesus' Name!

CHAPTER TWENTY-TWO

Poor Nabi

"He was despised and rejected by mankind ... we held Him in low esteem." Isa. 53:3 (NIV)

Our new kitten, Nabi, is the cutest thing! She's gentle and playful and wouldn't hurt a flea. A kitten's never been on anyone's list of "things to be feared," but you wouldn't know it by the treatment she receives around here. Rocky, our senior cat, despises her! He constantly hisses and bares his fangs. Nash avoids Nabi like she has the plague, and yet he doesn't mind stealing from her bowl. Most of the time Ed ignores Nabi or barks like an old grouch. Why can't they show her a little kindness or something in between indifference and hatred? Why are they all so mean to this sweet, harmless cat? I think they may be jealous of the attention she's getting from us.

I've often thought about why people treated Jesus so terribly in His day. Perhaps it's because He went against many social norms and especially elevated women and children; treating them with respect and allowing them to listen to His teaching along with the men. He tirelessly fed the needy and healed the sick, those everyone else ignored. Foreigners and outsiders were welcomed by Him, rankling the "pure bred." Maybe it's because He wouldn't bow to their agenda and use His powers to end the corrupt Roman government (His plans were better — He wanted to remove corruption and sin from every person's heart.) He stepped on self-righteous toes. People had no tolerance for talking about their own sin. They wanted a little god they could control and keep up on a shelf — one that would judge others, but not them.

Even Jesus' critics admit He was a great humanitarian, gifted teacher, and impeccably moral man. It's perplexing that the so-called religious leaders decided that this model citizen needed to be crucified — a punishment reserved for the worst criminals. It's troubling that it didn't even faze them to watch Him be brutally tortured and hung naked on a cross. It had to be something much more sinister than just a jealous power grab.

Jesus lived and died over two thousand years ago — it doesn't make sense why the unexplained, irrational contempt continues. What inspires such bizarre expressions of vitriol, such as the horrid crucifix submerged in urine, on display in "art galleries" from NYC to Paris? And why don't we use the names of indisputably evil men — like Hitler or Stalin — when we smash our fingers? Why not, once in a while, use another so-called deity for our expletives like, "Confucius damn!" (or occasionally exclaim, "OMC!")? Undoubtedly, the prince of demons continues to inspire worldwide hatred for a humble "Man" who lived over two thousand years ago. Satan has always been jealous. He wants us to worship him (or one of his guys). He loves it when we despise (or just ignore) the true God. Bible writers foretold exactly how Jesus would be treated over 700 years before He came in minute detail.[21] It is unarguable proof that Jesus is who He claimed to be — the Son of God!

---

[21] Isa. 52:13-15, 53:1-12. (NIV).

CHAPTER TWENTY-THREE

Bellyaches and Heartaches

"There is a way that appears to be right, but in the end it leads to death." Prov. 14:12 (NIV)

I put out Nash's supper, and he just stared at his bowl with apathy. I hadn't seen this behavior since we started making his food. When Nash first came to live here, it took him the whole day to eat one bowl of dried dog food. His stomach stayed in an "uproar." We could hear it six feet away. His gassy eruptions sent us running from the room. The vet ordered lab work, stool samples, and meds, which may as well have been placebos. We bought every kind of food, from cheap to high-end, grain-free, organic, and gourmet. Nash turned up his nose at Every. Single. Thing.

I started researching dog food and found it shocking to learn about the many recalls for several different brands. It was distressing to read about the incidence of pets getting cancer, diabetes, and other things, possibly related to their food. The ingredients on many dog-food packages were lacking and vague. I had nothing to lose and formulated a recipe. Nash gobbled down his new food like a teenage boy with hollow legs! Best of all, there was no more "spin cycle" in his tummy and zero runny stools!

So, this morning, I became worried when Nash lay there limp as a dishrag, refusing to take one bite. Then I remembered deer season is in. I am sure Nash supplemented his diet with something gross he found in the woods. I wish I could convince him of the direct correlation between his foraging and his bellyaches.

I poured my heart out to a young woman recently who told me she was moving in with her boyfriend. I explained that it was a recipe for disaster, that romance usually ceased, resentment would build as she constantly auditioned to be his wife. I told her God's warning, that *unmarried sex has great potential to harm your whole being.* (1 Cor. 6:18) I explained that God didn't want to see her heart broken or for her to experience the associated chaos. I shared with her my own mistakes and the regret that still plagues me years later. I begged her not to listen to the false message of the culture, that says, *"Have safe sex!" (But how do we guard our hearts?)*

God never meant for sex to be dangerous — and it isn't when it's protected in a committed loving marriage. People encourage cohabitation, and say, *"It's best to try each other out,"* like they're test-driving a new car! But the truth is, these couples will be "putting nails in the coffin" of their marriage (*only half will make it to the altar*). Their "noncommittal-commitment," is fragile. Statistics reveal they're raising their odds for divorce higher than average, (some studies say as high as double).[22] Couples who cohabit report increased depression, fighting, and a five times higher rate of separation. Children raised in these homes have a higher incidence of psychological problems.[23] I pray she has the wisdom to see the direct correlation between today's choices and her and her children's future well-being. God was so kind to give us such fatherly instructions that give us a much better way to a happily-ever-after.

---

[22] Scott Stanley, G. Rhoades. Premarital Cohabitation is Still Associated with Greater Odds of Divorce.10/17/18. Institute for Family Studies, https://ifstudies.org/

[23] Marripedia.org/Cohabitation and Future Marital Stability.

CHAPTER TWENTY-FOUR

Rescuers Rescue

"Since we have now been justified by His blood, how much more shall we be saved from God's wrath through Him." Rom. 5:9 (NIV)

Recently, I was getting ready to decorate a cake. I left the kitchen for a second but covered the bowl of icing tightly with plastic wrap and pushed it to the back of the counter-top, so Nash wouldn't be tempted. When I returned, I found my bowl of pink icing on the floor! Thoughts of trading him for a short-legged Dachshund were running through my head. Lucky for Nash, Serenity happened to be home, she jumped in to rescue him. She kept saying sweet things to defuse my snit, *"He can't help it ... he's just a dog ... look how cute he is."* While I was cleaning up the mess, she was working hard as the goodwill ambassador between us.

When our daughter, Jordan, was a little girl, she rescued a half-dead mouse from the claws of our hungry cat. Jordan took the initiative and created her own plan of care. She sprayed antiseptic on that poor little mouse to ease its pain, then attempted to blow air into its mouth with a medicine dropper. The mouse succumbed to its injuries, but not for lack of trying on Jordan's part. (Fun fact: Jordan just graduated from medical school this past May!)

My own rescue story started when Ray and Joyce Kluttz drove to Florida from North Carolina to receive guardianship of me and my brother (age 5 and 6). My birth-mom had called her cousin, Joyce, begging her take the two of us; we were living in horrible circumstances. Ray and Joyce's teenage son, Banks, went into a back bedroom and scooped up my infant sister who had just awakened (that they did not know about). Banks brought her outside where we were loading the car and asked if she could come too? Our bio-mom said, "Oh God, you want her too?!" (And they did!) My life went from bleak to blessed, with great parents and an awesome big brother! (Banks was our bedtime storyteller, activities director, etc. etc. And my kids have had a crazy-fun uncle!)

Jesus is the ultimate Ambassador of Peace and Rescuer. He rescued a woman who was caught in the act of adultery and was about to be stoned for it according to the law of Moses. (John 8:1-11) A mob of angry men were circling when Jesus intervened. I believe Jesus' words convicted them of their own lustful hearts, because not a stone was thrown that day. Jesus knew He would soon be taking every sinner's punishment on the cross, so He stepped between her and judgment a few days early.

Jesus came to save sinners from their slavery to sin and from the judgment to come. The Father planned our salvation, and then sent Jesus on the rescue mission. God is holy and pure love; He despises sin for how it hurts us and wrecks the world. The Bible warns that unrepentant sinners actually store up God's wrath against themselves. (Rom.2:5) But Jesus was willing to go to the cross as a shield between us. His proxy punishment is enough to satisfy God's righteous anger for every sinner and every sin. But it's only those who repent (are willing to give up their sin) and believe God (will forgive them because of Jesus' sinless life) who will be shielded from judgment. God is the Judge, and His beloved Son acts as the Defense Attorney for believers.

CHAPTER TWENTY-FIVE

Skunked Again!

"... the Holy Scriptures are able to make you wise ..." 2 Tim. 3:15 (NIV)

Nash tangoed with a skunk again last night! I knew it as soon as I opened the door to the porch to feed him breakfast. Maybe Nash was running away; the hit wasn't as bad as the last time. But that's like saying this breakup, or audit, or fracture wasn't as painful as the prior one. I'm really bummed — the odor from his other interaction had just worn off. The consequence of Nash's behavior was now my problem to solve. So, I made a concoction of peroxide, baking soda, and baby shampoo from the stockpile I'd kept from the last go round. I followed the "online expert's" instructions to a "T." No matter, the acrid odor remained intractable and pungent. I was disappointed, I don't know why I held such high expectations — it didn't do much (if anything) the last time we tried. The anonymous gurus also suggested bathing Nash in minty mouthwash if plan A failed. That suggestion left me feeling somewhere between skepticism and gullible. Maybe I'll try it tomorrow. In the meantime, I hope Nash figures out those adorable little critters are not in any way fun playmates. Interestingly, old Ed has never had a single run-in with a skunk. I wonder where Ed obtained his wisdom — perhaps his poppa-dog gave him the rundown. Maybe Ed can teach Nash? But the "rank" reality remains — my silly Nash has a penchant for skunks, and until the odor lessens, we cannot be close.

God not only sent Jesus to set us free from sin and judgment, but He provided specific instructions on how to really thrive while we walk with Him. We don't have to flounder in confusion; His priceless counsel is free and available in the Bible. God's Word covers every topic, and it's timeless for all generations — like good medicine — when applied daily to one's heart, it heals your soul. God takes a holistic approach to our well-being. Following His imperatives, like choosing to forgive, and being sober and self-controlled, will definitely facilitate better emotional health and often improve physical health. When I made Jesus King of my life, and started taking His Words seriously, my world went from complete dysfunction to ever-increasing stability. Much-needed changes started occurring in my character, which greatly improved all my relationships. Friend, I have never regretted a single day of being a Christ-follower. Life with God at the center, works!

I've seen my adult children apply God's wisdom in their lives as well. It is absolutely clear that the more they follow God's ways, the more they bless the people and the world around them. My daughter, Jordan, answered God's call to manage a Kenyan orphanage at age 19. During that time, she went to God in prayer for everything. Our daughter, Song is only twenty-five, yet wise beyond her years. She chooses her friends well and dates a guy who cherishes her. She lives simply; because of her self-discipline, Song is able to help others financially. She is a talented graphic artist and is always making the world around her more beautiful. (She designed the lovely cover of this book!) My daughters consistently start their days by reading their Bibles and seeking out God's sage life instructions. I believe this habit has made all the difference.

CHAPTER TWENTY-SIX

'Nashing Through the Snow

"The Lord your God is with you, the Mighty Warrior who saves. He will take great delight in you; in His love He will no longer rebuke you, but will rejoice over you with singing." Zeph. 3:17 (NIV)

We woke up to our first snow of the winter with temperatures in the teens. No matter, I decided to layer up and go walk. I looked like a polar bear waddling around. Nash plodded sleepily from the garage, sniffed the white powder, then flopped down with all four legs splayed out. He rotated like a skewered marshmallow and writhed around to get his back side completely coated. Nash seemed to relish his snowy bath! He turned to his tummy; like a sniper, Nash inched forward and plowed the snow with his snout. Nash opened his jaws like a front-end loader and attempted to chew the powder. He leaped up and ran off like a spastic reindeer, then turned back zigzagging toward me, signaling that he wanted to play chase. Nash made indescribable and delightful doggie noises that made me laugh so hard!

My bulky winter gear hindered me from taking off after him. So instead, I collected handfuls of dry snow to throw at him. It was breathtaking to see the showers of iridescent diamonds raining down all around him. Eventually, Nash enticed me into a game of chase; but first I had to shed a few layers, so I could keep up with my young, fun doggie playmate.

❄ ❄ ❄ ❄

There's an amazing love story in the Bible. The true story began with an older woman, Naomi, and her daughter-in-law, Ruth, both having been widowed and thrown into extreme poverty. Ruth "happened" to scavenge for food at the farm of a distant relative — kind, wealthy, eligible — Boaz. Every burden tumbled off their shoulders after Boaz married Ruth. Naomi gained a son-in-law, grandson, laughter, and hope. Ruth got a loving husband, who gave her a future and everything she needed. (Ruth 1-4)

Jesus is Boaz, my sweet Savior and Soulmate — the True Love I had been looking for in all my past relationships. His love for me is still a mystery — I had nothing to offer Him — but all He wanted was my heart. When you come into an unbreakable, covenant relationship with a promise-keeping, never dying, eternal God, so many burdens leave. No more fear of death or judgment will leave lots of room for peace and joy. Plus, you'll have extra energy and mental capacity to show up for a purpose-filled life. Without the ball and chain of sin and shame weighing you down, you can run and play like a child again. I feel much younger than when I was twenty-something!

CHAPTER TWENTY-SEVEN

Stinging Flies

"So in Christ we, though many, form one body, and each member belongs to all the others." Rom. 12:5 (NIV)

Ed is a very calm, laid-back, yellow lab. He was sauntering out in front of me with his tail going like a windshield wiper on low when suddenly he became a completely different dog. Ed started leaping, snapping, and going in circles — all at the same time! My mellow dog was acting more like a jackrabbit at this instant. Then I saw the cause: there on Ed's back was a large horse fly. Ed scared it away with all his gyrations, but as soon as he settled down, that old fly began harassing him again. I called Ed to come near me, so I could defend him. Poor Ed was working so hard to keep it at bay that he didn't hear me. That pesky fly was like a bad dream, it kept coming back. All by himself, Ed could do nothing to stop it from stinging him again. So, I hurried over to him, instead of waiting for Ed to come to me. I waved my arms like a ninja on steroids over my pitiful dog. My technique may not have been pretty, but not a single horse fly bothered Ed as long as he stayed close to me.

I hate how a perfectly lovely walk with my dogs can be ruined by negative thoughts. Usually there's a thread of truth, which makes them more difficult to fend off. I've learned it's best to act quickly and take control of my thoughts by directing them to something positive. I usually just start singing, praying, or saying Scripture out loud.

Years ago, I had a freaky incident that I had no experience or context for. I was driving by myself on an errand when a heavy depressing emotion enveloped me. My mind was suddenly bombarded with harassing thoughts: *I was not loved, nor needed, and I'd be better off dead.* I started weeping uncontrollably. But God's Spirit spoke to my heart: *turn on the radio.* It was preset on a Christian station; praise music flooded in. I was no longer alone — there was a whole church choir inside my car! I've always heard that demons flee when they hear God praised. Whatever it was, left immediately.

I've found there's another great help for battling darkness: it's when I call on my sisters-in-Christ to pray over me. Their faith boosts mine when I'm running low; then other times they need me. There's always supernatural power when God's people meet together. We gather so often that our church friends are more like family. We've celebrated each other's kids' weddings and helped carry each other through funerals. We take casseroles to the sick and pass the hat when someone's struggling. Friend, life is the sweetest in God's community! Please accept your standing invitation. Go become a part of God's family — you've not fully lived till you've heard a well-timed sermon; unburdened at the altar; sang praises with abandon; or enjoyed a potluck on homecoming Sunday!

P TWENTY-EIGHT

Nash's Treasure

"For where your treasure is, there your heart will be also." Matt. 6:21
(NIV)

I fed Nash breakfast today, and his dreadful breath made me recoil. When I went back out to walk later, Nash came running over with the source of his halitosis — a half-eaten old rabbit carcass dangling from his mouth! I was relieved when I saw him go bury his "treasure" in the yard and hoped he'd forget about it. But later, I noticed Nash in his doggie-bed with his bloody "snuggle bunny" tucked up close to his side. We feed him very well, yet, he remains hopelessly attracted to rotten things. I dread it, but I'll have to glove-up and steal his nasty "prize" before it makes him deathly ill. His dead things must go if he treasures time with me.

⁂

I recently read about a young man who left the faith. His reasons were that God was cruel for allowing Jesus to be crucified. It was his opinion that God made too big a deal of sin. I once turned away, too. My excuse was that God's demands were impossible to keep. (That was by design — to drive us to call on Jesus.) Granted, I had some valid theological questions that needed to be sorted out, but my true motive was I loved my sin more than God. We all worship something; mine was the unholy trinity of — me, myself, and I.

But God stepped in and rescued me. I was actually relieved when I found I could stop trying to be good on my own and trust Jesus to make me brand new. I found unbelievable rest when I gave up trying to win the sin struggle in my own power and let the Spirit do the work. God actually changed me from a sin-lover to a lover of Him. Now I see clearly that God is loving and wise — life done His way works well. Hindsight is 20/20. I can look back and see how sin grows until it takes over our lives.

I once worked as a nurse on a bone marrow transplant unit. Often patients died, not from the cancer directly, but from the side effects of the harsh treatment regimen. The somber reality was that the remedy had to be lethal to eradicate the killer-cancer cells. I never once thought the doctors were cruel but recognized their stringent protocols were the only hope to extend my patient's life. However, I did learn to hate cancer as I witnessed its greedy devastation. I wonder if this illustrates how God feels about sin. I now get the necessity for the cross — it took Jesus' death to conquer sin and death for us. The Father dearly loves His Son, if there had been any other way to save us — He surely would have arranged it.

Sin brings death, and it's a worldwide pandemic; as a result, ten out of ten people die. But people still reject God's remedy — the Savior, Jesus Christ! But friend, the cure is as close as a sincere prayer to offer yourself to God. Then you can really start living with your God-privileges through Jesus. The blessings are too numerous to count and so amazing that they're hard to believe. There's salvation from sin, release from guilt and judgment; no fear of death, adoption into God's family, an inheritance equal to Christ's, and a forever-home in heaven waiting. We are loved greatly, and nothing will ever change that. Jesus and the Holy Spirit pray for us 24/7. The Spirit is available to help us with anything and everything, at any time. We are given access to over 5,000 Bible promises. It would be insane to reject this good God! I've been walking with God for almost thirty years; I've found that He's the greatest Treasure in heaven and on earth.

CHAPTER TWENTY-NINE

Funniest Thing

"A cord of three strands is not easily broken." Eccl. 4:12 (NIV)

I scheduled a nature photographer to come to the house to photograph my husband and me with our pets early Sunday morning — 6:30 a.m. to be exact. This was the only "prime time" where our calendars would intersect, and there'd be "soft lighting and no shadows." I was super worried how the day might go due to the crazy time, among other things: my husband would just be getting off of a 24-hour shift, I would be arriving home late from a long road trip, not to mention that *certain members* of our family have a history of being grumpy on "normal" picture days. Would the dogs want to sleep in, since they chase deer all night? Hopefully, the cats wouldn't hide. This morning had lots of potential to be a waste.

My sweet man was very gracious the whole time! However, halfway through the session, both our faces showed our fatigue. The photographer said, *"Think of the funniest thing you've ever seen."* I immediately whispered a recent incident to my husband. A huge grin spread across Bob's face and all the way to his twinkling green eyes. He was pleased to share the memory with the photographer. Last week Bob had grabbed some scrubs straight from our dryer and carried them to work. Upon changing in the men's locker room, he found a pair of my old granny panties stuck with static electricity inside his scrub shirt. Bob had to work to regain his composure before starting surgery. There was no more need for our photographer to say, "Smile!" and the pictures turned out great!

Jesus went to a wedding where they ran out of wine. His mother asked Him to correct the situation. He sped up time and made aged wine. Plain water was turned into the best vintage they'd ever drank. Everyone praised the groom for being so generous. (Jesus' work often makes us look good.)

Jesus saved the day for my marriage as well. We knew we were running short on all kinds of vital things, like faithfulness and patience. We turned to Jesus in the first year of our marriage. That decision saved us from our destructive ways. God started transforming us and removing stubborn attitudes that were robbing us of marital peace. God was our source for love and forgiveness — He never ran out.

I think Jesus enjoyed the reception and didn't want it to end. God loves our marriages, and it breaks His heart when they grow cold. He invented marriage and knows how to make them thrive. We need only to ask, like Mary did. Then God enters in and does a miracle to keep them sweet and strong. He's been the "third strand" holding Bob and I together for twenty-nine years. We still get sideways every now and then, but God is right there as referee and counselor all in one. No doubt, it has been God that has been gluing us together — He deserves all the credit and praise!

CHAPTER THIRTY

Stop, Drop and Roll

"The Lord is good to those whose hope is in Him, to the one who seeks Him." Lam. 3:25 (NIV)

Nabi has figured out how to get our attention. We can't help but notice her. When we walk outside, she runs over and stops, drops, and rolls onto her back right at our feet. We have to be vigilant so as not to step on her. It's so endearing that I can't help but stoop down and love on her. Her purring elicits such happiness from me and sounds like a *"Thank you!"* She's the most relational cat I've ever seen. Nabi even takes walks with me and the dogs. (I usually carry her part way.) Nash started copying her. Now I stop to pet him, too. He could stay there all day and doesn't move a muscle or hardly breathe. The only thing Nash lacks is a doggie-purr; I'm pretty sure he smiles at me.

🐾 🐾 🐾 🐾

A favorite Bible character of mine is Daniel — a young man who was able to thrive, in spite of being surrounded by evil in really crazy times. Daniel chased after God, remaining loyal to Him no matter the cost. Being second to the king surely kept him busy, but he made time to pray — Daniel stopped and dropped to his knees three times a day! The other officials were jealous of his high position. They worked to outlaw prayer. No matter, Daniel kept his vital appointments with God. As a consequence, he was thrown into a lions' den. However, Daniel had the divine favor of the King of Kings. We don't know exactly what happened, but the lions either got sleepy, or (for the first time ever) lost their collective appetites. (Dan. 6)

A few years ago, I mentored a precious single mom. We met regularly over lunch for two years. Ten years earlier her ex-husband had an affair, and then abandoned her and their two toddlers. She shared her many struggles with me. Her finances were stretched thin. One day, she animatedly informed me the dentist had just told her that *both kids were going to need braces soon.* She almost shouted, *"Where will that money come from?!"* I was probably grandstanding when I responded, *"God will provide!"* I believed all the stories of how God rescued people way back in Bible times. But I really didn't have faith He would intervene, definitely not in this situation, braces are cosmetic and not really necessary. I poured out my heart to God; it was mostly a complaint about the unfairness of it all. I'm sure she called out to God daily and as often as she cried.

A year later, this same friend's ten-year-old daughter won an essay contest. *The prize was free braces ... The contest was sponsored by a local orthodontist!* My friend recently remarried, and I had the pleasure of making her wedding cake. The King of Heaven still blows our minds and gives special favor to those who come near and stop to pray.

CHAPTER THIRTY-ONE

Trees, Marvelous Trees

"They will be called oaks of righteousness, a planting of the Lord for the display of his splendor." Isa. 61:3 (NIV)

I started late for my walk this morning and was wilted in the summer sun before I had gone a hundred feet. Nash and Ed trudged along beside me in solidarity; their limp tails revealed their misery. I wanted to return to my air-conditioned house, but the sight of the lush oak trees up ahead beckoned me onward with the promise of shade.

Trees showcase the wisdom and kindness of God so well. God truly blessed us when He gave us trees. They do so much to enhance the world and provide a multitude of things: paper, pencils, tissues, tables, chairs, pianos, guitars, doors, floors, sailboats, fruit, and nuts. Trees fuel our fires and stabilize our walls. They make secure homes for critters and birds. They beautify our landscapes and filter carbon monoxide from our air.

Jesus' life here on earth could be described as a metaphorical tree. Like a willow with low-hanging branches, His outstretched arms welcome all who come to be saved. He halted His sermons, so children could climb Him like a cherry tree to be near His heart. He was as unchanging as an evergreen in that He never tired of doing good or talking about the Father's love. He had the strength of an oak and never once gave into sin, lust, or hate. Like a tree cut down for pulp, Jesus gave everything. How ironic, then, that a life-giving tree was forced by men to be a hideous instrument of death. But God redeemed that tree, too, and it became a beautiful symbol of life: a wooden bridge between us and Him. What would the world be like without Jesus — the epic Giving-Tree?

Jesus described His Father's kingdom as a little mustard seed that, when planted in a humble heart, has all the potential to mature us into someone wonderful — much like the life-giving tree described in Luke 13:18-19. God loves to do such unlikely, mind-blowing things that start out subtle and unseen. Jesus began His life here on earth as a tiny embryo growing silently in the womb of an awkward teenage girl. And God's message spread through the world without radio, social media, or cable TV. Jesus took on the identity of an outsider — a poor, uneducated carpenter's son. Yet with His death and resurrection, Jesus was like a huge redwood — felled by demons, but in the end, it crushed their evil king.

This pattern is repeated every time God starts faith-seeds sprouting inside a heart. His Spirit empowers us to grow up to be like Jesus: lay down our lives, pick up our cross. We minister to the broken and push back darkness while God's kingdom spreads. We reflect Jesus' love every time we offer food, shelter, or shade to the needy. May we live like trees with purpose, and keep our arms, like branches, lifted high in praise of our King.

CHAPTER THIRTY-TWO

God Interrupts

"A new command I give you: Love one another. As I have loved you, so you must love one another." John 13:34 (NIV)

My sweet dogs don't seem to notice when I'm distracted and hurried on our walks, but I feel bad even so. Today was that kind of day without any margin. I got up extra early and was rushing to get in my three laps. I was halfway through lap one when thoughts of my friend "Kay" came to mind. She was scheduled for surgery today; I knew she had been apprehensive about it. I felt God urging me to stop and go message her. I turned back to the house. I sent my version of Psalm 121 to encourage Kay:

"Dear Kay, God never sleeps ... He watches over you constantly ... you can go under anesthesia without any fear ... God won't blink, won't nod off, or take His eyes off you until your surgery is through."

I found out later that Kay was, at that moment, overhearing the anesthesiologists outside her door voicing their concerns about her chronic breathing problems. Needless to say, this compounded Kay's already anxious thoughts. She made a swift decision to cancel surgery and started getting dressed. My text came through at that moment, and Kay's husband quickly read it to her. She was immediately filled with supernatural peace! Kay's new confidence came because she knew God had noticed her struggle. God's perfect timing coupled with the powerful words of Psalm 121 filled Kay with the assurance of God's loving presence. She lay back down on the gurney as serene as a child resting in her Heavenly Daddy's arms.

God's call to "*lay down our lives*" will always be at least a little inconvenient. It often interrupts our plans and requires a sacrifice. It cost Jesus His life. God uses this to mature us and to showcase His character in the world. God sees suffering and injustice and responds through His servants of mercy. He calls us to suffer with them as we become His tangible hands and feet. Once you get involved in God's service, you'll realize He cares about every single soul. His knowledge of our circumstances will blow your mind and build your faith. God is so intimately involved, He even "*knows the number of our hairs on our head.*"[24] Serving humanity for this gracious, kind God will fill you with joy and awe.

Jesus told a story about a traveler who came upon a nearly dead man lying by the road. The traveler interrupted his plans and spent his own money to save the stranger's life.[25] Jesus traveled to earth to meet our needs. He rescued us from eternal death and paid all the expenses with His blood. Every time we pause to help another, we're reenacting that beautiful story in some way. Only a good God would have chosen, "*Love your neighbors*"[26] as the number one behavior to characterize His people in the world.

---

[24] Luke 12:7 (NIV).

[25] Parable of the Good Samaritan; Luke 10:25-37. (NIV).

[26] Mark 12:31 (NIV).

CHAPTER THIRTY-THREE

Unreachable Itch

"But whoever drinks the water I give them will never thirst. Indeed, the water I give them will become in them a spring of water welling up to eternal life." John 4:14 (NIV)

We took Nash to the groomers for the first time in three months. It was the end of summer after he'd been running through the creeks and fields. He looked like a Bohemian with bur-filled dreads. The groomer certainly had her work "cut out" for her. Stephanie definitely gave us our money's worth (or maybe it was revenge)? Our newly shaved Nash was as close to naked as a dog could possibly get! His ears were buzzed close as suede shoes. The only vestiges of his old self was a round puff ball at the end of his tail, which curled up and acted like a feather duster mercilessly tickling his rump. When we were out walking later, Nash stopped every few feet and went into a spasm. He contorted into a pretzel in an attempt to scratch his own back with his teeth. Of course, he couldn't reach it no matter how hard he tried. Then he rolled around in the grass for momentary relief. I saw his misery and paused to scratch his itchy hindquarters for him. When I realized how much he enjoyed it, I rubbed all the way up to his shoulders and back down. Nash stood there like a statue getting a massage. I'm sure Nash would love to be able to reach every inch of his body the way our cats can. Maybe this is why our cats don't need us as much as the dogs do?

There's a Bible story of a man named Zacchaeus, who was employed as a wealthy tax collector. He had made his money by shady means. Jesus was in town and surrounded by a crowd. "Zach" was curious to see Jesus, but he was a short man, so he climbed up a tall tree. Of course, Jesus noticed and came to the exact place beneath Zach's perch. He called Zach down and later ate at his house. Zach was so moved that he was reborn and transformed instantly! This once stingy thief immediately volunteered to give half his savings to charity and to repay four times over what he'd taken dishonestly. Jesus had "hit the spot" in Zach's heart. (Luke 19)

A huge part of God's call is for His people to be generous with their time, money, and praise. Before I met Jesus, my selfishness was like poison ivy of the soul. My unrelenting "pruritic passions" were self-preservation and self-promotion. But since Jesus came into my life, He's reaching the "itchy spots" that keep me hoarding and boasting. He's removing my fear of not having enough and my insecurity and pride. There's such deep soul satisfaction and contentment as He fills my emptiness; there's no room for anything but His love and joy. Now, I can't stop singing His praises!

CHAPTER THIRTY-FOUR

Walking Pets

"Let us run with perseverance the race marked out for us, fixing our eyes on Jesus, the pioneer and perfecter of faith." Heb. 12:1-2 (NIV)

The two cats joined the dogs and me on our walk this morning. After about twenty yards, both cats got tired, then stopped, and sat down, right in front of my feet. When I went to go around Rocky, he leaped up like a hobo hopping a train and wrapped his four legs around one of mine! Gravity took care of that rotund cat for me. Old Ed's legs don't go very fast, and he trailed behind. Even with his arthritic hips, he insists on coming along. Nabi and Rocky left us and went back to doing whatever cats do. Of course, the cats can't go the distance — they don't have the legs for it. Only dogs can enjoy long walks with their friends.

🐾 🐾 🐾 🐾

My childhood church tradition made me aware of the holiness of God and acutely conscious of my sinfulness — which is true and vitally important. However, I don't remember God's grace being mentioned; His love seemed to belong to a few who attained sinless perfection. Salvation was a gift, but we had to work to keep it. There was ambiguity about which sins, how many, or just one, would "null and void" our good standing with God. I kept backsliding in my spiritual game of *"[Shafts] and Ladders."* Our theology was missing key ingredients, like eating cake without the oil and sugar. I had fleeting moments of sweet peace with God. It was enough to keep me striving to try to please Him, but eventually I ran from Him.

There was no peace apart from God either. So as a wife and new mother, I realized I desperately needed God. He led me to Chapel Hill Bible Church, where the pastor kept referring to us as "friends" and taught the whole Bible and full gospel. The theme of grace was repeated over and over. Salvation was based solely on the perfection of Jesus and the good work He'd already completed. I learned the point of salvation was to display God's amazing attributes. Only by God's grace are we saved, and it's by grace we continue growing. Salvation is a no fail proposition; God fills us with His powerful Holy Spirit the moment we believe in Jesus. The Spirit adds whatever we need and gradually removes anything that hinders our walk with God. God saves us ... then keeps saving us. Our part is just to give ourselves to Jesus.

When I stopped trying to save myself and started trusting Jesus to do it, I was able to rest in His sweet love. Now, there's no fear of Judgment Day because I know Jesus has already taken my sin and punishment. The trial is now rigged in my favor: Jesus' perfect record will be read instead of mine; He will be my Defense Attorney, and the Judge is our loving Father-God.

CHAPTER THIRTY-FIVE

Dog Perfume

"Look after each other so that none of you fails to receive the grace of God. Watch out that no poisonous root of bitterness grows up to trouble you, corrupting many." Heb. 12:15 (NLT)

When we lived in town, we had wonderful next-door neighbors. There was just one little annoying problem, and I didn't say anything for the longest time. But my frustration grew until, one morning, I went right over — all red faced — and told them exactly what was on my mind. We had a small adjoining yard where our children played, and we daily walked through. They had two indoor dogs, and when they took them out to do their "business," it seemed it was usually right smack in the middle of our intersecting yards. They had a large garden space in the back and a sizable front yard, too, but the dogs got to "choose their spot," and their preference was right beside us. (*Now this was before I became a dog lover.*)

I remember the incident painfully well. We were leaving for school, and the three kids and I hurriedly jumped into the minivan and slammed the doors closed. Before we could buckle up, I knew that someone had come in contact with a fresh "doggie-pile." The offending pair of shoes happened to be mine. Something this foul coming from a nearby cow pasture might be tolerable, but NOT when it was following me around attached to my shoes. I took them off and left them in a bucket of water and bleach. My temper could have ruined our friendship, and my attitude was stinkier than "doggie-do." But they forgave me, and we all remain good friends.

This event reminds me to be careful not to leave hurt and anger stewing because there's no way to know the exact point where unforgiveness morphs into toxic bitterness and then destroys us. It's been often quoted, *"Holding onto a grudge is like drinking poison and waiting for the other person to die."*[27] I have seen firsthand a loved one choose this path. As their bitterness consumed them, they lost their mental and physical health in a slow suicide. If only we'll pray and release it to Jesus, He will enable us to erase all records of wrongs. God in His wisdom commands us to forgive without counting and to do it quickly until it is our default position. The sad alternative is a heart wound that will fester and ruin our souls. Jesus set the ultimate example by praying (while hanging battered and naked from a cross), *"Father forgive them, they don't realize what they've done."*[28] This kind of Savior is able to heal all heartaches and even remove a stronghold of bitterness if we'll but ask. He will exchange them for His redeeming love, which stays behind like a sweet perfume and fills our hearts with peace. Then there's no room for anything inside us except His goodness and grace; they will overflow from us as fragrant forgiveness for even our enemies.

---

[27] The Sermon on the Mount: A General Introduction to Scientific Christianity, by Emmet Fox. (Harper and Rowe, New York, 1938), 99.

[28] Luke 23:34 (NIV).

CHAPTER THIRTY-SIX

Look at My Dog!

"... go and make disciples of all nations, baptizing them ... and teaching them to obey everything I have commanded you." Matt. 28:19-20 (NIV)

I loaded up the car with Serenity and Nash to take her to school. As we pulled into the drop-off lane, she observed a schoolmate exiting his car. Serenity was always looking for any opportunity to show off Nash. She loved him so much. He was her rock star! So of course, Serenity rolled down her window, hung her body half out, and yelled, *"Look at my dog! Do you want to see my dog?!"* The teacher allowed the boy to walk over with her. Ms. Jenny did her best to corral Nash to the backseat. Serenity made the introductions, and a doggie-kid love fest ensued. Other cars were arriving, so the teacher quickly shooed the kids into the school. I'm confident those two started an unofficial Nash Fan Club that day.

In the first century, Jesus left His band of seventy followers with the mission of telling others about life with Him. In spite of persecution, their message was compelling and spread like a wildfire throughout the Roman Empire. For almost three hundred years, there were no churches because Christianity was illegal; believers met under the wire, in houses and hidden places. They shared the message of salvation and caught the attention of unbelievers with their joy, their kindness, and their stable families.

The Romans were ripe for a Savior and a new way of living. Society was riddled with lawlessness, alcoholism, incest, and open marriages. Rome's worship of pleasure and violent entertainment left them bored. The news that Jesus would satisfy was welcomed.

Through the centuries, authentic followers of Jesus contributed to their society's well-being. They made a positive impact on the culture by loving their neighbor and doing good with the intention of making God famous. Christians started innumerable charities, orphanages, adoption agencies, schools for the poor, and even invented the first hospitals in God's honor.

Americans have religious freedom and churches everywhere, yet believers are not influencing the culture; now the culture is often dominating the churches. Jesus is not welcome in public places, and our society looks like the early Romans. People who identify as atheists have more than doubled in a decade.[29] Christians largely are keeping the good news to themselves. No one can deny the nation has nose-dived into chaos, and that unthinkable things are now common. We've just had the two most affluent generations of any time in history, yet the insatiable lust for more has so infected our nation that children are considered a burden, being sacrificed and trafficked. We've exchanged God's call to *"love our neighbor,"* for a mantra of *"doing whatever makes me happy"* — no matter whom it crushes. We need Jesus!

Friend, if you're not a believer, please investigate Jesus! Look for a joyful Christian and follow them to church this Sunday. Believers, it's okay to hope all our cars out front of our churches will cause passersby to become curious and want to come inside; but, we must shine our love-lights brighter out in the community and share the good news about Jesus, like the first Christians did.

---

[29] "U. S. Church Membership Down Sharply in Past Two Decades" by Jeffrey Jones. April 18, 2019; new.gallup.com.

CHAPTER THIRTY-SEVEN

Special Chair

"Let us then approach God's throne of grace with confidence, so that we may receive mercy and find grace to help us in our time of need." Heb. 4:16 (NIV)

Nash has his own wing back chair. I nabbed it for $20 from a thrift store and placed it on the front porch. This is his new favorite place to lounge and allows him to peer through the French doors at us, and us at him. It is really so endearing the way Nash loves to watch our every move. He's figured out where we'll be, so that is where he stays. His close proximity reveals he trusts that we will eventually notice him there. Nash doesn't ever go rest on the neighbor's porch. He understands that he belongs to us, that we take his needs seriously. We don't mind Nash's neediness; his complete dependence makes us only love him more. It was my original hope that by purchasing Nash a special chair and intentionally putting it right outside my door, my sweet doggie would choose to stay near.

❧ ❧ ❧ ❧ ❧ ❧ ❧ ❧

Even as a believer, I once saw the Bible as just a book of ancient history and moral laws. I had no idea it was a living book with supernatural power, but as a young mom, something dramatic happened to change my thinking. I found myself becoming over-the-top angry at my three kids! One day, I completely lost it and shattered a picture against a wall. I ran to my bedroom, fell across my bed, and wept in shame. God's Spirit didn't condemn me that day — *He said I could do better, and that He would help me.* The

Spirit instructed me to open my Bible and memorize Scriptures that addressed my anger and rage. Now God's words replay in my head when I'm feeling provoked; praise God, there's been no more tail-wagging-the-dog scenarios.

I too have a special chair where I daily share "coffee with Jesus" and read my Bible. This is when I deal with things like worry, bitterness, sin, and temptation. This practice has been amazing medicine for my soul! I battle A.D.D., and so I start by asking God to settle my brain and ensure that the time spent will not be "fruitless" or wasted. I pray through an acrostic that spells **FRUIT**. I ask for God's power to help me **FOCUS**, to **REMEMBER** His words, to help me **UNDERSTAND** what I've read. For God to **INSTRUCT** me on how to apply the truth and most of all, for Him to **TRANSFORM** me to be more like Jesus.

God also has a chair — it's called the "throne of grace." When we pray, we'll receive immediate attention, help, forgiveness, comfort, etc. There's no other place I know to go for the vital things I lack, like love, joy, peace, patience, gentleness, wisdom, and kindness. There's no other god that invites people to come close like our God does. Even when I wasn't coming near to Him, Jesus was pursuing me!

CHAPTER THIRTY-EIGHT

Who Is Walking Whom?

"As Scripture says, 'Anyone who believes in Him will never be put to shame.'" Rom. 10:11 (NIV)

My daughter Jordan and her husband, Ryan, set out on what they thought would be a relaxing ten-mile hike in the Ozarks. They had planned and budgeted for this mini vacation for a while. Of course, their two rambunctious, young Labradors were included in this family trip. After being penned up for three hours, the dogs were straining to run with the wind upon being let out of the car. Ryan held Piper's leash, and Jordan had Scout's. Jordan wrapped Scout's leash around her tiny wrist for good measure, just in case he had an irresistible urge to chase a critter. A mile into their trek, petite Jordan was still being dragged like a sled by Scout. She found herself literally "skating" on loose gravel as her feet lost traction — the dreaded moment had come when Scout spotted a squirrel *and Scout chased it right over a ledge!* Jordan was still tethered to her dog, and she helplessly sailed right over! Of course, Scout landed on his feet six feet below, but Jordan tumbled down the cliff and ended face down in the dirt. Scout's "leading" resulted in an Urgent Care visit, stitches to Jordan's bottom lip, and a vacation cut short. However, the worst part for Jordan was having to explain her appearance to her co-workers on Monday.

We're all born selfish due to our sin-natures. Our destructive "me first" impulses come from within and without. The culture glorifies selfishness. Individuals' "right to be happy" allows them to break commitments and break hearts, often leaving others in material and emotional poverty. For crying out loud, we live in the "selfie" age! Satan is behind this mindset and loves to watch as narcissism wrecks our relationships and our lives. But God offers us a double cure — a new righteous nature and His powerful Spirit inside. This new nature is so amazing — Jesus referred to it as being "born again" spiritually. We get a new spiritual DNA! We go from being the offspring of Adam to being children of God. We stop being rebels and start behaving like the obedient Son. When we let the Spirit lead, God promises to shield us from ever experiencing shame or regret again. God ensures you live a life of high honor, which He guarantees by filling believers with the Spirit — it's our soul's "ace in the hole." The moment we give ourselves to Jesus, the Spirit pours His love into our hearts and empowers us to live selflessly. The Spirit gives wisdom and enables us to avoid sin's collision courses, dead-end streets, and rabbit trails. God takes the most destructive sinners and turns them into productive citizens. Friend, I'm sure He can because He's doing it for me!

CHAPTER THIRTY-NINE

Traded for a Bone

"I know that the Lord is great, that our Lord is greater than all the gods." Psalm 135:5 (NIV)

Each morning, Nash always comes running and bouncing to greet me. I don't have to call him. Before I can get the door unlocked, he's on the stoop with his cute nose pressed to the door. But not today. Today Nash ignored me. He was nearby and playing with something. He kept grabbing the object of his affection in his mouth, throwing his head back, and tossing it into the air. After it fell, he quickly snatched it up again. I called to him, but he was so enthralled with this new thing, he never even noticed me. Not even a quick glance. I went over to investigate what I'd lost out to — it was last night's leftover beef-rib. And to think, I was the one who had given it to him! Nash was more interested in an old dry bone than he was in walking with me.

🐾 🐾 🐾 🐾
🐾 🐾 🐾 🐾

I have taken the good things that God has given me and turned them into idols, by loving them more than Him. When I fall madly in love with the gifts, I end up relegating the Giver to the periphery of my heart. The God who should be the center becomes just a "spoke on the wheel of my life." A bike missing a few spokes can keep rolling, but "hub-less wheels" fall off. Anything or anyone other than God can be taken from us in an instant. It's good and normal to enjoy God's gifts. But little gods are temporary and fail to deliver what we'd hoped; they often end up destroying us.

I poured myself into raising my children (a natural motherly thing), but I took it too far — obsessing over them took over my life. They felt pressured to be perfect as I put them on a pedestal. Thankfully, God showed me my mistake. By the time my "bonus daughter" Serenity came to live with us, I was able to keep everything in its proper place. I clung to Jesus but held onto Serenity loosely. I thoroughly enjoyed her; we had so much fun! It didn't destroy me when she was gone.

I realize now that only God can be God (and only He should be). God is Spirit, He's omnipresent, and won't move away. He's eternal and can't grow old or die. God alone is perfect and always exceeds expectations. He knows us completely and loves us unconditionally. His name is Faithful, He will never cheat or divorce us. There's no one and nothing else in the world that can fit that God-sized bill. Friend, just open your heart and give Him first place. It's like feasting at the ultimate Thanksgiving table; fast food will have no pull. When you're standing beside the ocean, making mud pies in the yard won't entice you. All God's good gifts on this earth are just glimpses of His amazing love; they're the little preview of heaven's joys. But the Giver cannot ever be replaced by His gifts.

CHAPTER FORTY

Why Worry?

"Therefore I tell you, do not worry about your life, what you will eat or drink; or about your body, what you will wear." Matt. 6:25 (NIV)

Nabi used to lie on her back in my arms like a baby and purr while I scratched her tummy, but lately she's been behaving strangely. But now she has started flipping around and *"hugging"* my shoulder with *all* her claws. All purring has ceased, and she acts like she's scared. Maybe she doesn't want to be put down, believing I won't pick her up again? Or possibly she's afraid I might drop her, and she must hold on? I don't know why she would think these things when I never have done either thing.

❧ ❧ ❧ ❧

Our family went to Mexico to build a home for a homeless family. On arrival, we realized my daughter's luggage had been left behind at a distant hotel. Kathryn's teenage heart saw this as *the end* of her life! We'd spent hours scouring the mall for one pair of denim shorts for Kathryn to wear on this trip, and she had carefully packed. Now, poor Kathryn had only the clothing on her back! The woman in charge there in Mexico, gave me a garbage bag full of donated clothes to look through. I just knew it'd be fruitless, probably old worn out garments and things that wouldn't fit her.

I need to give you a description of Kathryn for the rest of this story's full impact. Kat's two favorite things were music and sports. (She played school volleyball and summer league softball.)

She preferred wearing bright girly colors and bling, with one exception — her favorite "pajamas" were navy sweatpants and an oversized, sky-blue t-shirt.

The first item I pulled out of the bag was a large sky-blue t-shirt with a screen-print of the musical Jonas Brothers. There were a pair of navy sweatpants identical to the ones at home. (Nice coincidence.) There was a pair of modest denim shorts that fit her like a glove — but with rhinestones on the pockets. (Kat will *looove* this!) I found a hoodie in her size, from one of her favorite teen stores. (How lucky — this would be great for chilly mornings!) There were two perfect tank tops, fuchsia and bright orange, with sequins adorning the neck, that would keep her cool on hot days. (Now my mind was being messed with!) However, I wouldn't have believed the next items if I hadn't seen them myself. There were six t-shirts in Kathryn's exact size — all ladies' softball t-shirts from different colleges! (Okay, now I knew God was in on this!) We still have one that reads, "*De Paul Softball.*" There was not a stain or tear on these donated clothes; every single item fit my girl's body and taste. God is real, and He sees every detail of our lives. Friend, if God cares that much about a teenage girl's wardrobe, could you not trust Him with your whole life?

CHAPTER FORTY-ONE

Shuffle Your Feet

"You make known to me the path of life; you will fill me with joy in your presence ..." Psalm 16:11(NIV)

Nash loves to be chased. I love it, too. But some days I just "shuffle my shoes" on the gravel to make Nash think I'm coming after him. He takes off like a bullet without looking back, while I just continue on my walk. So far, this satisfies Nash. He's never tired of our game. Undignified snorting laughter usually erupts from deep in my belly as I watch Nash zigzag around. Our property is fenced in except for where our driveway runs through. Nash has always stayed inside the boundaries, except when a rare jogger or a stopped car is near. Unless I do something to distract him, Nash cannot resist going to check it out. I will grab his collar until the temptation passes, or I'll do the "shuffle" with my shoes, to get his attention back on me. At these times I really do chase after him with all my heart! And right toward the house and to safety.

Christians have all the best reasons to be the happiest people in the world. We are forgiven and adopted by God. He frees us from burdens like shame, guilt, and fear so we can really thrive. He gives us new vision to help us avoid the pitfalls that ruin people's lives. God shares His wisdom and character, so we can make good choices that lead to purpose and stability. He pours supernatural joy and new energy into our spirits allowing us to overcome daily challenges. God offers us wholesome pleasures that don't trap us in addiction, rob our health, or fill us with regret.

I once added up all the Sabbaths, holy days, and celebrations in the Old Testament. If spread throughout the year, the people of God had the privilege of resting and feasting with their loved ones every fifth day! God is a good Father who cares about His children. He gave us the perfect formula for enjoying sweet relationships and living fulfilling, productive lives.

God is supremely satisfied and happy. He invented laughter and reserved it for humans since we are made in His image. He loves seeing us joyful, and the Bible says that *glad hearts come from Him.* Some of the happiest, most content people I know are Christians. Our dear friends Robin and Dan could record and sell their amazing laughter. Mickey and Lucia never stop smiling. I know both of these couples have suffered big disappointments due to things beyond their control. And yet, they all are marked by extreme joy. Our kids' Aunt Bev buried the love of her life, Eddie, and became a young widow. No matter, she keeps serving people and Jesus. Bev has never lost her unique giggle and wonderful sense of humor. There's unavoidable suffering because the world is broken, but God's people have joy in the midst of the storms. It's because God showers us with His endless supply and keeps us satisfied with a purpose-filled life. And our Savior holds our attention as we dance together in the sunshine or pouring rain.

CHAPTER FORTY-TWO

Welcome, Stranger

"...Whoever comes to me I will never drive away." John 6:37 (NIV)

I noticed something recently, and the irony of it was lost on me until now. At the entrance to our driveway, we have two opposing signs side by side. One says, "Welcome," and the other reads, "ADS security." Our recent "guest" chose the first one as his cue. He came up onto the porch and made himself right at home. This visitor arrived sometime before daylight. I was in my favorite chair sipping my coffee, reading my Bible, when I looked up to see a large silhouette at my French door. I jumped to my feet and turned on the porch light ... whoa! Staring at me was a huge Pit Bull! Instantly, the recent news of a local man having been mauled by Pits raced through my mind. I needed to feed Nash and Ed breakfast, but I was too scared to venture outside. I studied all three dogs as they lounged together on the porch; they all acted as if this arrangement were normal, and there was no sign of a pecking order being established. (Maybe it's a given when you're his size.) Eventually, I found the courage to crack open the door. At once, there were three doggie-faces attempting to squeeze through. The new dog's tail seemed to be wagging in a friendly manner. I still wasn't sure if he could be trusted; it was crazy, but I stepped out. My knees were shaky, so I sat down in a chair. I was quickly encircled by a furry trio — none had any concept of personal space. Each vied for my attention all at once. The new dog came around to my left, with a flash he jumped up and put his front paws on the edge of my seat. He was huge before, but now he was immense! My heart skipped a beat. I'd never been near a Pit Bull, much less eyeball-to-eyeball. But not to worry, he started licking my cheek. I was soon "dripping" with affection by this stranger who was now welcoming me.

Jesus came to reconcile all people to the Father, to make us part of His family and share His inheritance. Jesus never met a stranger He didn't love, and He treated all people with dignity. He valued children and held babies with smelly diapers that leaked. He took heat for breaking "men only" traditions, by welcoming women into His inner circle, and inviting foreigners to help launch His ministry. Though He could heal by speaking, He habitually touched untouchables, diseased lepers, and such. He hung out with "big sinners" and never condemned them. The last thing He said to His followers was to reach out and include every race and nation to bring them into His kingdom.

There are no "Keep Out" signs, guard dogs, or fences with God. The only obstacles are on our side — fear, pride, unbelief. Turn all these things over to God. *Jesus will __never__ reject __anyone__ who comes to Him!* Let those ridiculously gracious words sink in. Has anyone but Jesus ever made such a declaration? Friend, if you feel the Spirit tugging at your heart, *please don't turn this kind, generous Savior away.*

CHAPTER FORTY-THREE

Brain Transplant

"I will give you a new heart and put a new spirit in you ..." Ezk. 36:26 (NIV)

Every couple of weeks Nash takes off and runs right to the neighbor's cow pasture. We dread it. When he returns, his blond fur has brown "highlights." Today was one of those days, and I didn't have time to bathe him. He had to remain outside; there was no petting him when we went for our walk together. He seemed confused by my strange attitude. Oh, I longed to be near Nash and to touch his sweet head. But I couldn't risk contamination with his germs or "barnyard perfume." I wish I could control Nash's urge to roll around in cow manure — maybe a doggie-girlfriend would inspire him to smell good? Why can't Nash think like our cats — they hate to be dirty. How about a cat-brain transplant? He'd be clean, but he would have a weird bark. I just have to accept this nasty habit as Nash's doggie-nature. He inherited it from his doggie-parents and just can't help it.

※ ※ ※ ※
※ ※ ※ ※

As a young mother, I became highly suspicious that all my children came into the world pre-programmed to be naughty. I noticed early on, when they got mad, they knew exactly how to show it. They threw impressive fits and deftly bit their siblings while grabbing handfuls of hair. They never attended a class on how to lie, roll their eyes, or sass me — they were all born naturals. I had to teach each one good manners — they came prepackaged with all the bad ones imaginable. I couldn't blame them, because they'd inherited my "spiritual DNA." I've also thrown notorious tantrums and told some whoppers in my day. I repeated plenty of my birth-mom's destructive behaviors, even though I wasn't raised by her.

A Bible character, Abraham, started a family tendency for lying. "Abe" told a "white lie" to protect his own skin. He misrepresented his beautiful wife as "just his sister" (which resulted in her being kidnapped twice)! Abe's grown son, Isaac, did the exact thing in response to a lusty king who noticed his pretty wife. The lies got bigger with each ensuing generation. Isaac's son, Jacob, pretended to be Esau and stole his brother's inheritance. Years later, Jacob's sons cruelly convinced him that his son, Joseph, was dead (when they knew he was alive). (Gen. 12-37)

God redeemed the whole family of Abraham. He rescued the ladies from the harems and turned Abe into a valiant fighter. He refined Jacob's character, healed his rift with his brother, and gave him back his beloved son, Joseph!

Joseph is a beautiful representation of Jesus. Like Jesus, Joseph was sold by his brothers who hated him. Yet, Joseph forgave and saved them from death. He brought peace to their dysfunctional family.

Jesus offers to pluck us out of our toxic bent that we inherited and passed down to our children. He is willing to graft anyone into His perfect family tree and give us all a new righteous heritage. A decision to follow Jesus will bring you a new heart and greatly bless your future generations.

CHAPTER FORTY-FOUR

Dogs Face East

"Christ was sacrificed once to take away the sins of many; and he will appear a second time, not to bear sin, but to bring salvation to those who are waiting for him." Heb. 9:28 (NIV)

When Bob steps outside in the morning, the dogs are waiting at the steps. He is usually in a hurry, and there's not time for petting, but these four-legged groupies are content just to see their rock star's smiling face. The dogs watch their favorite truck go down the winding driveway until it disappears. They walk with me later, but other than that they spend most of the day sleeping. Ed prefers the garage, and Nash the front porch. They occasionally awaken to roam the yard or to check for a missed morsel in their bowls. Nash often explores the woods or plays chase with the neighbor's calves.

But you can set your watch every afternoon around four o'clock. Both dogs will be stationed in the front yard, lying side by side, always facing east, staring at the entrance to our driveway. These former sleepyheads are now fully alert, as if they were guarding Fort Knox. Even before they can see Bob's truck, they can hear the sound of his tires on the gravel. Then they leap to their paws and start running to greet him. Ed is magically transformed into a much younger version of himself, and for a short distance, he keeps pace with his young companion. Nash is beside himself with glee to see this spark in his old pal. He cannot resist this opportunity to play.

Nash runs in circles around old Ed while they simultaneously race downhill. The whole way down, they each have a signature bark they reserve for such happy times as this. It's an amazing display of affection as they welcome their beloved Bob home. The feeling is mutual, and Bob often stops and loads them into his truck. Nash prefers to be inside; Ed loves the truck bed. They both bark to high heavens all the way up the hill. They know a treat is awaiting them from Bob's leftover lunch.

＊ ＊ ＊ ＊
＊ ＊ ＊ ＊

The Bible gives a limited description of Christ's physical departure from the earth. The angels in attendance told His friends that He would be coming back the same way. No specific date is given, but there are certain conditions that would be present on the earth. Biblical prophecy describes a world characterized by people rushing around, a rapid increase in knowledge,[30] self-absorption, hedonism, extreme greed, abuse, violence, family conflict, wars, disloyalty, scams, severe weather, natural disasters, hyper-anxiety, and pandemics — to name a few.[31] One doesn't have to be a Bible scholar to see these things are presently here.

Jesus said there will only be two categories of people when He returns: those who love Him and those who don't. There's no third category for the indifferent. We were all His enemies at one point, but Jesus died to make us His friends. The invitation still stands for all who sincerely call upon Him. He promised to reward His friends (those looking for Him) with eternal life on the new earth.

---

[30] Daniel 12:1-4 (KJV).

[31] 2 Tim. 3:1-4 (NIV); Luke 21:10-11, 26. (KJV).

CHAPTER FORTY-FIVE

What's Got Into Him?

"Every good and perfect gift comes down from the Father who created all the lights in the heavens." James 1:17 (CEV)

I had just gotten back home after being out of town for a few days. Ed and Nash were extra excited about going on our walk. Nash bounced all around. They ran out ahead of me, like it was a race. Their tails were wild, wagging in celebration, beckoning me to catch up with them. Then suddenly, Nash ran off into the grass. Unexpectedly, he turned around and charged like a bull toward me (imagine a cute, white, fuzzy, friendly one) heading for the matador's cape. I thought, What in the world?! and braced myself for impact. But when Nash was at arm's distance, he zoomed to the right. He romped away, then turned on a dime and came back again — this time he headed straight for Ed! I giggled and wondered what was going to happen? Was this a game of chicken? Or would lanky Nash try to tackle stout, old Ed? I stopped in my tracks to watch the action. Ed stopped, too; he was real plucky, holding his ground. At the last second, Nash feinted left, missing Ed by a few hairs! Stoic as stone, Ed appeared unfazed and unimpressed as Nash galloped by. I wouldn't have believed it if I hadn't seen it ... but Ed slowly turned his head and looked over his shoulder at me. His expression, if I could read it, said, "Crazy kid ... What's got into him?" I laughed till I shook. I thanked God who made them for me.

God is the greatest Giver! He's provided countless things for our pure enjoyment. Instead of creating one bland food as fuel for our bodies, God made all kinds of textures and flavors, then gave us taste buds. God designed a kitten's purr and equipped the birds to sing — for our listening ears. He was surely thinking about our children's toes and sandcastles when He invented sand. God used the whole color spectrum when He decorated our world with flowers, birds, and much more. He mesmerizes us with such varied land critters and crazy sea life. People spend lifetimes studying all of it.

However, in my opinion, dogs are the most amazing and fun creatures! These gentle canine companions really showcase God's extreme kindness to us. God's generosity ensured they'd be ubiquitous and accessible to everyone, no matter how poor. Dogs love us so well; they often put us humans to shame in that they're faithful till death. God didn't have to create dogs for us; they aren't necessary like oxygen or food. We could live without these four-legged friends — but only if we had to.

All of these gifts are just tiny expressions of God's grace, compared to the gift of His Son! Friendship with God, through Jesus, is so ridiculous and astonishing — it's hard to believe! But when I look around at how God lavishes us with His love in so many extravagant ways, it brings me to a place of unwavering faith.

Friend, if you feel God's love drawing you, don't resist — you're just one prayer away from your whole world being wonderfully transformed! Believe that Jesus is real; that He loves you and died in your place. You can trust Him with your burden of shame; confess your sin directly to Him. Don't worry about saying the "perfect prayer." Just speak from your heart and give yourself to Him with all that you can. Life will start making sense — He'll guide your life, and fill you with His wisdom, goodness, and amazing love.

CHAPTER FORTY-SIX

When Fear Fades

"Jesus immediately said, 'Take courage! It is I. Don't be afraid.'" Matt. *14:27 (NIV)*

Nash and Ed constantly wander off to go "leave their mark" or to follow a scent. It's such a common occurrence that I don't pay any attention to it. This particular morning, Nash ran to a ditch and started barking for all he was worth. His whole body was pricked. He kept inching forward, only to leap backwards again. I wondered if his objective was to intimidate whatever it was, or if he was actually plotting a supplemental meal. Whatever the case, I continued on past and chose to ignore all this doggie-drama. I walked to the end of the driveway and then returned to where Nash was holding his lone vigil. His normally short attention span was unswerving. My curiosity was piqued, and I went to investigate. Old Ed followed suit. When I saw it, wow, was I impressed! There were goose bumps covering my arms. It was scary and fascinating all at the same time. Ed and I backed up in unison. Nash seemed emboldened since we were now there. But he didn't touch it — he was wise enough to realize we three were no match for this monstrosity in the grass. This guy held sway over his domain and appeared to be enjoying himself, completely at ease — it was the largest snapping turtle I'd ever seen! We gave him no reason to pull inside his shell or sneak away. He had our deepest respect, and there was zero chance we would advance an iota past his invisible line in the sand.

COVID-19 is wreaking havoc across our globe, instilling unbelievable fear. I usually ride every wave of panic — but not this time. God intervened. Just before the COVID crisis started, I "happened" upon a book by Andrew Murray on divine healing that I didn't even know I owned. I found it in a drawer where I usually keep photos. It's as if Jesus spoke straight from the pages to my soul. As I read, I found such courage. Mr. Murray pointed out Bible promises that emboldened me to pray more for healing miracles. He reminded us that God can do today what He did in Bible times. That Jesus still saves spiritually and physically; He conquered death and is the source of eternal life. Nothing is impossible for our great God![32]

God knew how scary life here would be, so He wrote words of comfort for us. Someone counted and found 365 times in the Bible it is written, *"Do not be afraid."* Jesus went to a lot of trouble to save us from sin and fear and so much more. Nothing in all creation scares Him. And fear fades when you spend time with Him. He showed up and saved the day — when the waves were highest, food scarcest, and after the patient had already died. It's intentional and by God's design to strengthen our faith and to ensure it's in Him alone. Jesus always had enough courage to go around back then; He still does today. I've found supernatural calm in Jesus to face this new invisible enemy. Christians can face every fear with divine strength — because the Author of Life is our Father, Christ is our Savior, and the Holy Spirit our constant Companion. Friend, I've experienced it in my life over and over that God is faithful, *"You cannot trust Him too much!"*[33]

---

[32] Andrew Murray; Healing Secrets (Whitaker House, New Kensington, 1982), 17-52.

[33] Healing Secrets, IBID, 145.

CHAPTER FORTY-SEVEN

The Hardest Lap

"I have fought the good fight, I have finished the race, I have kept the faith." 2 Tim. 4:7 (NIV)

When I step out in my tennis shoes in the morning, my dogs go crazy. Words from their mouths would be completely redundant as they wag all over to express their delight. They always take off ahead of me, but on returning back up the hill, I'm usually in the lead as their enthusiasm wanes. Today, Ed knew his limit and plopped down in the shade after lap one. Nash only made it through two. On lap three, they had both thrown in the towel.

So, I walked the last lap alone and was having a typical conversation with God. Then out of nowhere, the most incredible joy came sweeping over me! God's presence was more tangible than the ground beneath my feet. I almost floated along in His sweet love. In a holy awe, I laughed and cried happy tears while whispering, *"Thank You, thank You, I love You, I love You, God!"*

I still wonder why God chose to surprise me with a taste of heaven that day — and if or when He'll do it again. Maybe it was to remind me, *I'm never alone.* Or to encourage me for some difficulty that lies ahead.

This last half of life has been harder than I expected, yet strangely, very satisfying and sweet; God has been faithful and close. These years are marked by grief for the passing of many loved ones and the bittersweet ache of an empty nest — but the "God of all Comfort" has been true to His Name. I spent many futile years trying to "fix" certain relationships. God finally convinced me to let go — now there's so much more peace. God gave me the wisdom not to waste any more time on frivolous and fruitless pursuits. I'm better now at following His lead to invest in people and meaningful endeavors that are eternal. The ravages of time are displayed in the mirror, but God's affection has never waned; every birthday just brings me closer to seeing Jesus! God's grace has allowed my husband and I to reap sweet fruit in our marriage after years of hard work. When thoughts of being widowed or diagnosed with a terminal illness nag me, God repeats He will never leave me; that He will walk through every moment with me. Chronic insomnia should leave me drained, but God lets me draw from His endless well of energy. After praying certain prayers for the hundredth time, God finds ways to show me He's listening and working out every detail according to His perfect timing. I get discouraged that I still struggle with selfishness and ugly sins. But God reminds me how far we have come from where He found me — that I don't have to be perfect, because Jesus' blood and righteousness covers everything. God whispers to keep trusting Him. He promised that we'll finish this last lap together. My faith might "flicker" every now and then, but God will make sure it sustains me until the very end.

Friend, God wants to walk through life with you, too. From the core of my being, I promise — you will never regret a day with Him in it! God is real, and He is good. He loves you more than you can ever imagine.

How to give your life to Jesus Christ

Think of it as making a wedding vow to the greatest love of your life! It's a pledge of trust and a lifetime commitment. It's the start of a relationship and an adventure you will never regret!

A Sample Prayer:

Dear Lord Jesus,

I believe that You are the Holy Son of God; that you took the wrath of God for my sin on the cross; that you rose from the dead to give me eternal life. Please make me born again now, with a new spirit and heart to obey you. By faith, I receive you, Jesus, and your pardon, your cleansing, and your goodness into me. I take you now as my King. Make me part of your kingdom and family. Fill me with your love and power, so that I can really love you and my neighbor. Thank you for your plans to save me daily from my sin habits and selfish ways. Thank you for your promise to keep loving me forever. Lead me to a community of believers, so I can learn your ways and grow in faith. I give you my heart and life from this day forward.

In your Name, Jesus. Amen.

If you prayed to receive Christ today:

Tell a friend.

I'd love to hear from you at darceysbooks@gmail.com.

Strengthen your faith: Read the Bible daily. Talk with God and pray throughout your day. Connect with a Christian community and get baptized. Worship God by helping someone in need.

Be blessed!

Darcey Beale

JOYFUL, JOYFUL, WE ADORE THEE

Joyful, joyful, we adore Thee, God of glory, Lord of love;
Hearts unfold like flowers before Thee, opening to the sun above.
Melt the clouds of sin and sadness; drive the dark of doubt away;
Giver of immortal gladness, fill us with the light of day!

All Thy works with joy surround Thee, earth and heaven reflect Thy rays
Stars and angels sing around Thee, center of unbroken praise.
Field and forest, vale and mountain, flowery meadow, flashing sea,
Singing bird and flowing fountain call us to rejoice in Thee.

Thou art giving and forgiving, ever blessing, ever blest,
Wellspring of the joy of living, ocean depth of happy rest!
Thou our Father, Christ our Brother,
all who live in love are Thine;
Teach us how to love each other, lift us to the joy divine.

Mortals, join the happy chorus which the morning stars began;
Love divine is reigning o'er us, bringing all within its span.
Ever singing, march we onward, victors in the midst of strife,
Joyful music leads us sunward in the triumph song of life.[34]

---

[34] Words: Henry van Dyke, 1907. Music: Ludwig van Beethoven, Symphony No. 9, 1824. public domain.

Photos

Ed and Nash sit in anticipation of a doggie bone
(Kathryn Beale, photographer)

Waiting for Bob to come home (M. Sutherland, photographer)

Rocky is benched (Chu-Young Kim, photographer)

High grass & misdemeanors (Chu-Young Kim, photographer)

Baby Marie - definition of cute

Scout & Piper (i.e. the Cocoa Pups), dreaming of birds and squirrels (Barbara Smith, photographer)

Sleepyhead Nash

Nash & Serenity play dress up

Ed resting at the feet of his hero

Ed & Kathryn share a tender moment (Chandler Thornton, photographer)

Ed patrolling the grounds (B. Moore, photographer)

An empty nesters' family photo (B. Moore, photographer)

Faithful Ed (B. Moore, photographer)

Family photo on Easter Sunday

Foofoo Nash (a rare moment)

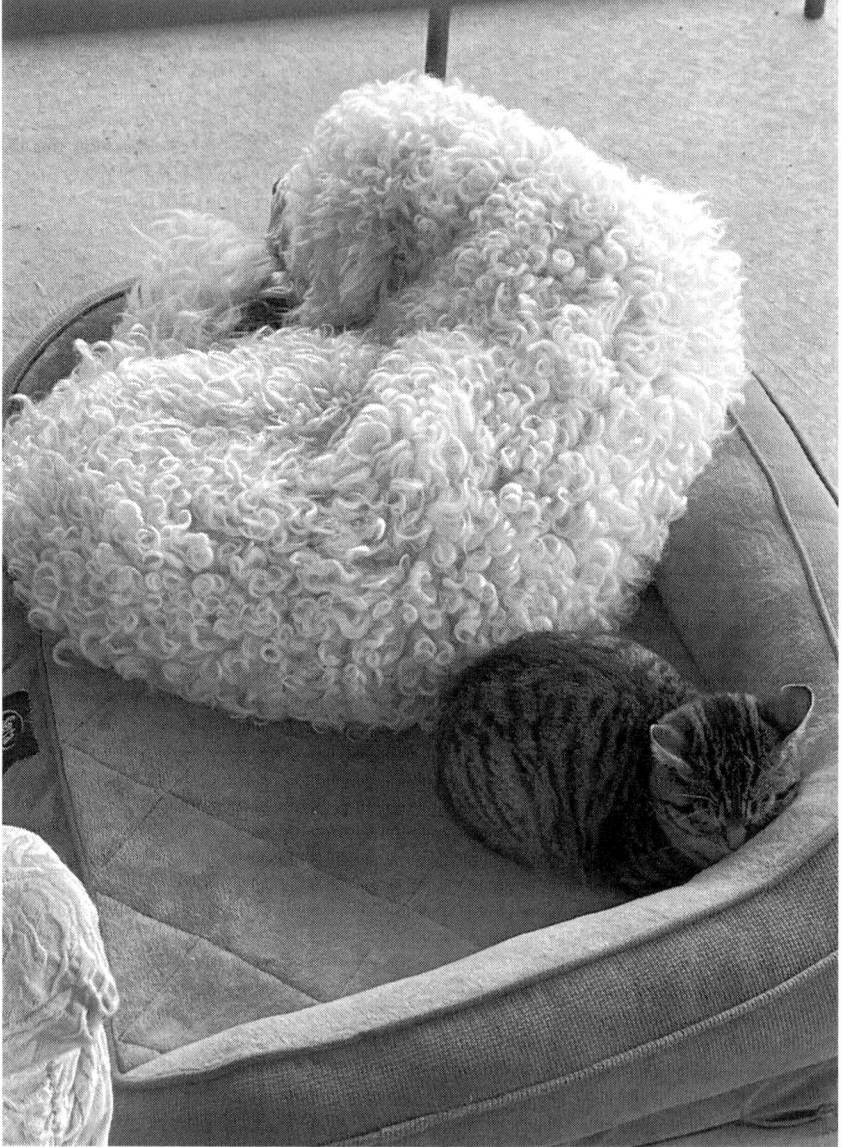

Nash & Nabi call a truce

Nash gets busted

Comfort food for a comfort dog

Incognito Nash

Nash receives TLC from Jeremy

Nash & Ed are the welcoming committee

Have you seen my copy of The Dog Street Journal?

Nabi's tummy-rub roll

Flower child in the Black-Eyed Susans (Mickey Sutherland, photographer)

Serenity…

Nash & his Cockleburs

Security Blanket

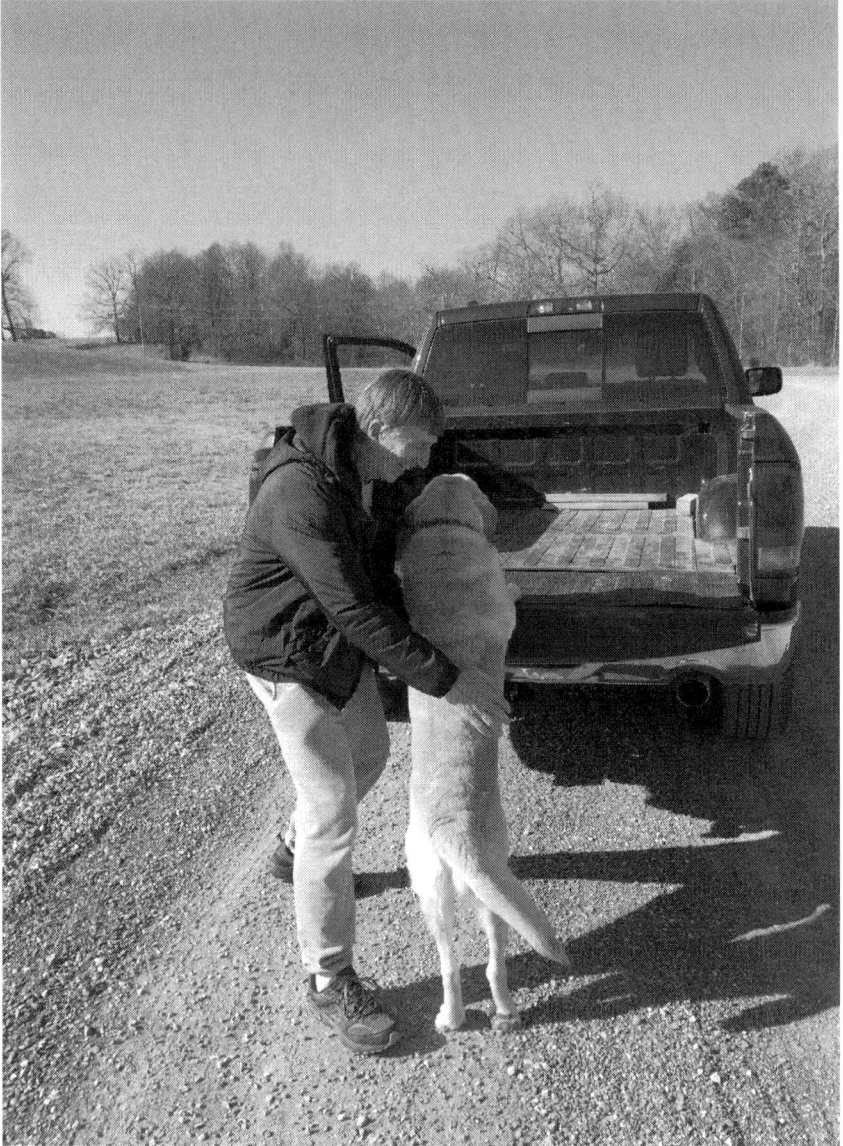

Ed gets a lift onto their truck

Ed takes a selfie

My name is Nabi (Korean for butterfly)

My name is Nash (short for Nashville)

My name is Rachmaninoff, but you can call me Rocky

Nash likes Darcey's chair too!

Let's go for a walk! (B. Moore, photographer)

ACKNOWLEDGMENTS

My heart is overflowing with gratitude for my sweet man, Bobby Beale! Without him, this book wouldn't be here. He insisted I attend the writer's conference, where the seed grew. Bobby "picked up my slack" at home and massaged my neck as I typed. He never criticized, but "spoke the truth in love" as my first-round editor. I could never have done anything good enough to deserve him.

(Two years ago, I wouldn't have said it) but thank you darling daughter, Kathryn, for "loaning" Nash to me and affording me much belly laughter and joy. Thanks for commenting on every, single dog-story and not being embarrassed to forward them to your friends. (It meant the world!)

Thanks dear daughter Song for designing the book cover; for sharing your creative input and gifts.

I'm beyond thankful to my parents Ray and Joyce Kluttz who adopted me from a hell hole! That one act removed a million barriers that I was born into and gave me as many reasons to thrive.

I've been so blessed by my big brother, Banks — my first and favorite storyteller! He stoked the fires, by making a big deal about everything I wrote.

Much gratitude to my lovely friend, and fellow dog-lover, Kim Davis — this book was her idea. She bought me a journal to write my dog stories in. Her encouragement along the way was oxygen to my soul.

What would I do without dear friends, Lucia, Rita, Robin, Julie and Brandy, praying for me?! How lost would I have been without Mickey and Janece's expertise and help on the computer (that I hate)?!

If I'd made a list of characteristics for the perfect editor — it would've described Beverly Beale. She's both a dog-lover and a lover of God. Bev's great sense of humor helped her understand my quirky mind-set. On top of all that, she's a brilliant English teacher. Bev loved me so well with her gentle corrections, copious affirmation, and generous gift of time. I'll never, ever get over it.

Thanks to my doggie-companions, Ed and Nash, for walking with me every day and inspiring me.

These dogs and loved ones are just more evidence of God's kindness and love for me...

good dogs: GOOD GOD

Made in the USA
Middletown, DE
02 December 2020